Successful Leadership
in the Early Years

Successful Leadership in the Early Years

June O'Sullivan

B L O O M S B U R Y

LONDON · NEW DELHI · NEW YORK · SYDNEY

Featherstone Education

An imprint of Bloomsbury Publishing Plc

50 Bedford Square
London
WC1B 3DP
UK

1385 Broadway
New York
NY 10018
USA

www.bloomsbury.com

Bloomsbury is a registered trademark of Bloomsbury Publishing Plc

First published 2009 by Continuum International Publishing Group
This second edition published 2015 by Bloomsbury Publishing Plc

British Library Cataloguing-in-Publication Data
A catalogue record for this book is available from the British Library.

ISBN:
PB 978-1-4729-1903-8
ePub 978-1-4729-1905-2
ePDF 978-1-4729-1904-5

Library of Congress Cataloging-in-Publication Data
A catalog record for this book is available from the Library of Congress.

1 3 5 7 9 10 8 6 4 2

Typeset by Newgen Knowledge Works (P) Ltd., Chennai, India
Printed and bound in Great Britain by CPI Group (UK) Ltd, Croydon CR0 4YY

This book is produced using paper that is made from wood grown in managed, sustainable forests.
It is natural, renewable and recyclable. The logging and manufacturing processes conform to
the environmental regulations of the country of origin.

To view more of our titles please visit **www.bloomsbury.com**

Contents

Introduction

This book has been written for those early years leaders currently working in this sector. Early years covers a range of settings. Being an early years leader means you could be leading a school, nursery class, private nursery, voluntary-sector nursery or children's centre, or be the leader of a room, group or team. In fact, the term 'early years leader' is very versatile. In this book, I have used the term 'leader' to mean all or one of those roles, so that you can apply it to your particular situation and take from the book what is most relevant to you. It is only in Chapter 9 that the early years leader is a specific role as the focus is on supporting the board of governors or trustees, and this is mostly the responsibility of the head teacher, the chief executive or the director – the person, irrespective of their title, who is in charge of the whole organisation.

The book includes self-evaluation tasks and activities to use with staff teams, either as part of their training or in a staff meeting as one way of encouraging talk, peer-to-peer support and reflection – a key constituent of a quality setting.

The activities are designed to encourage thinking by asking questions about how you or staff members would respond to a situation. They are also written to provoke your understanding and knowledge and test your own learning, or to transfer your ideas to staff as a means of checking their understanding and embedding this in practice. So often I thought I had shared an idea, only to find some time later that what I thought I had said was interpreted quite differently by the staff. A message can be very easily distorted on the short journey from articulating it to implementing it. In addition, people's learning styles have a significant impact on how they assimilate information. Kinaesthetic learners appear to dominate in early years and that means new ideas, initiatives or changes need to be introduced in such a way that people can use all their senses to examine the idea and fathom how best to respond and make the idea work in their setting. Each chapter also has a section called 'Think and reflect!', intended to encourage you and your colleagues to step back and consider what is actually happening, rather than what you would like to be happening.

I hope that this book gives some indicators as to what helps us to lead successfully, including sharing the lonely challenges all leaders face so you do not feel so alone and can learn to congratulate yourself on personal successes.

1 The journey to successful leadership

Successful leadership is credited as a key element of a good setting. This is both exciting and uplifting, but it also presents a personal challenge for each of us to examine why we lead, how we lead and if our leadership is good enough to make a positive difference.

Despite its recent popularity, the notion of leadership still remains something of a mystery. The definition of leadership is not conclusive and is perhaps best described by Bennett et al. (2003, p. ix) as 'a contested concept'. The current leadership debate highlights the complexity of the role, which in turn reflects the complexity of the sector. The one common message that has significance is that good leadership makes a difference, and effective and knowledgeable leadership is critical to the success of early years settings. Studies produced since the 1990s have reported that the quality of programmes and services for young children and their families is related to how the early childhood centres are led. Capable and responsible leadership is one of the most important reasons identified in determining the most and least successful children's settings and services. Leaders of ineffective settings are more likely to be inexperienced leaders, and this is manifested by their inability to develop their staff, encourage partnerships and make the service central within the community.

The importance of good leadership is also noted by Ofsted in many of their annual reports, most recently in 2013–14, and considered a very important central feature of a high-quality service. Harris et al. (2003) referred to similar research in a range of educational contexts which revealed the powerful impact of leadership in securing successful organisational development and change. Studies that examined low staff turnover pointed to positive leadership and, in particular, the leader's ability to involve staff in decision-making, although this is only part of the story. It would therefore seem that leadership has a significant part to play in the success of organisations.

Why lead?

According to Kotter, leadership is very challenging. He pointed out that:

> *Providing effective leadership, at least in big jobs, is rarely easy. If it were, we would see an*
> *abundance of good leadership throughout history. Indeed, even in the simplest conditions a*

variety of things are needed to create the vision and strategy and to elicit the teamwork and
motivation. But simple conditions are not the norm any more. Complexity is the norm.

(Kotter, 1988, p. 28)

This is certainly my perception, especially on days and weeks when there is no let-up and one challenge follows another without reprieve, and I ask myself for the umpteenth time why I or anyone else would want to be a leader!

Clearly, people become leaders for different reasons. Some people lead because they have a vision they want to share and bring alive, or they have a drive to make changes and lead new initiatives. Others have leadership thrust upon them because they were in the right place at the right time. More prosaically, sometimes people are next in line in a situation where they are moved up the ranks in an ordered hierarchical manner, and eventually find themselves at the top. I have met people who are still surprised after months and years that they have been officially crowned the leader of the organisation, the team or the group area. For those of us working with children there appears to be an urge to get it right for the children and create an experience that will translate into meaningful and rational practice. We also want to create and develop learning organisations where staff are supported in becoming reflective practitioners and action researchers, to help shape and grow high-quality services.

The words of Adair emphasised the democratic principle of leadership and that we lead together, not alone:

[T]he truth has become increasingly clear that a democratic society does need good leadership.
For leaders enable free and equal people to be effective in doing what needs to be done. The
principle applies to every organisation and institution within democratic society.

(Adair, 2002, p. 335)

Counter that with what Marconi said:

Nearly all tyrants began as popular leaders and often they were trusted because they spoke out
against the distinguished.

(Guglielmo Marconi, 1874–1937)

It's a salutary thought and it is worth recognising that not all leaders are good people or remain good people, although they may have set out as passionate and positive leaders who wanted to make a difference for people.

"Leaders should never, ever try to look cool – that's for dictators." (Ben Elton, quoted in Ratcliffe, 2000, p. 218). Remember this salient point when you wield power in your organisation, and keep in mind that what you do as a leader can actually make a difference between a child's – and an adult's – failure and success.

The emerging early years leader

For those interested in leading the early years, it is worth remembering that in the recent past, educational leaders were more often praised for effective management of the budget, the organisation and the political conditions. Just as in other fields, leadership and direction were the key elements that drove either good or bad organisational performance and leaders were measured against the successful delivery of organisational objectives through careful management of systems and information, structure, processes and people.

Nowadays, there has been quite a shift, and leaders in early years are expected to make a significant impact at many different levels, including helping address social injustice by ensuring key government initiatives (such as the free early education entitlement programme for two year olds in 2012) are led effectively within the varied range of early years settings. The Organisation for Economic Cooperation and Development (OECD) 'Starting Strong II' report in 2006 highlighted the benefits of investing in well-led services, particularly in the light of research from Field (2010), and this was reaffirmed in the 'Doing Better for Children' report in 2009 and 2011:

We have found overwhelming evidence that children's life chances are most heavily predicated on their development in the first five years of life. It is family background, parental education, good parenting and the opportunities for learning and development in those crucial years that together matter more to children than money, in determining whether their potential is realised in adult life.

(Field, F., 2010, *The Foundation Years: preventing poor children becoming poor adults*)

Countries should invest more resources early when outcomes are more malleable and foundations for future success are laid. If well-designed, universal interventions concentrated early in a life cycle can enhance both social efficiency and social equity. All children may be aided, but benefits may be greater for those who are most disadvantaged in the first place. Concentrating investment early means that it is also most likely to be effective in breaking the dependence of children's outcomes on those of their parents – intergenerational inequality – which is a widely held concern in many countries.

(OECD, 2009, *Doing Better For Children*, p. 16)

Children from disadvantaged backgrounds who face higher risks across their life cycle can benefit more from greater spending. Policy can ensure that later investments in high-risk children complement risk-loaded investments in the same children earlier in their life cycle. Early successes for such children should not be allowed to wither on the vine.

(OECD, 2009, *Doing Better For Children*, p. 16)

Early years leaders are increasingly held accountable for optimising later-life chances, equality of opportunities and the route out of poverty through the quality of education, care and learning provided for children, families and the community. This was reaffirmed in the 'Doing Better for Families' report in 2009:

> High quality early education: attending a high or medium pre-school has a lasting effect in promoting or sustaining better social behaviour outcomes, in terms of increased 'self-regulation', higher 'pro-social' behaviour and lower 'anti-social' behaviour levels at age 11.
>
> (Sylva, K. et al. 2004)

It is a serious agenda and one that can weigh heavy. We need to be prepared, not just by understanding the impact we can have but for how we can achieve this in complex and – at times – taxing circumstances. For example, in early years we continue to operate within continual change. During the last 20 years in the UK there have been over 100 separate Acts of Parliament affecting children.

In addition, by placing so much emphasis on leadership and consequently making it appear complicated, and virtually unattainable, it seems that, unless we are superheroes, it is almost impossible to lead. In fact, leaders in the sector are not heroes but ordinary, modest people who, through exceptional commitment, effort and determination, have become extraordinary. It reminds me of the television programme *The Secret Millionaire*, where each week a millionaire finds, to their surprise, that there are many ordinary, quiet, self-effacing people who are doing extraordinary things that make a significant difference to others. Early years leaders are among those great and quiet people. We must learn to be less quiet about being extraordinary.

The leader in action

The title 'leader' places a number of unconscious expectations on anyone aspiring to, or occupying, the role – not least the idea that leaders are inspirational and motivational, that they have a sense of purpose and direction, and that they bring with them an aura of power, capability and vitality. In reality this can set people up against impossible expectations with a high risk of disappointment. It must be like meeting someone famous you admire in real life and discovering they are shorter and more haggard than you could imagine. Disenchanting all round! Successful leaders seem to be able to do three things: behave in a particular way, have an ability to understand the needs of people and circumstances, and apply certain leadership styles at the right time. Good leaders appear to have acute self-awareness and understand the ideals that many people associate with the role of leader, and can pre-empt how they will react. Understanding yourself and being tuned in is a great start.

This book focuses on issues of leadership in organisations, particularly early years organisations, but I believe it is wise to learn from the research and experience of those in other sectors too. While organisational context is very important and an area we explore in more detail later in the book, considering research from more generic leadership also adds value. Not so long ago, Gallup conducted a very large leadership study asking 8,000 managers from 400 companies what they thought great leaders had in common. Published by Curt Coffman in his book *Break All the Rules* (1999), the findings appeared to indicate that great leaders do not have all that much in common. However, it was noted that a significant similarity was the way great leaders treated people. They recognised their different skills, abilities and motivations and didn't fall for the view that, with a bit of training, everyone would be the same; in fact, they talent-spotted and tried to fit the right person to the right position, helping the best performers to the right role rather than just getting poor performers to perform better. Good leaders came across as people at ease with themselves, who recognised their own strengths and weaknesses and fitted themselves into the right positions. They looked for ways in which their natural talents could make the big difference, while also replicating this process with others around them. Successful leaders seem to be people who have a high level of emotional intelligence and are aware of themselves, the people around them and the task they have to complete. They also seem to manage to combine their personal self-awareness and social skills with the ability to manage themselves and keep their emotions and impulses under control. There has been other research which has suggested that the best leaders are choosers who continually develop themselves and make new opportunities, while less effective leaders deny and ignore opportunities. American executives who were asked 'What do you look for and admire in your leaders?' produced strikingly consistent answers in surveys over a period of seven years. According to Tomlinson (2004), successful leaders care for their people. They do not need training to convince staff they care. They also care deeply about their work, and this means that their 'genuine care balances the respect for individuals with the organisational task. Caring may take some detachment to see the whole picture and take tough decisions.' (Tomlinson, 2004, p. 119).

I believe that an effective leader is someone who is able to share a vision which shows staff where they fit in, so that everyone has a sense of purpose and worth and can find their place in the organisation. Leaders need to get things done, make change happen and evaluate successes and failures with honesty. To be a successful leader you need to have stamina and energy and enthusiasm. You need to be able to go the extra mile. Not many of us have met successful leaders who spend their time complaining and whinging about their lot. That is what you do with your friends over a glass of wine, not in front of or to your staff. Leaders need to be pragmatic so they can overcome unnecessary barriers in order to change and make improvements. When Maria Montessori was looking for a way to improve the lives of poor children in Naples, she set about finding them a place that gave them warmth, food and order before she got them learning. Leaders need to be able to influence and negotiate at every level, from sorting out a problem with fees to negotiating a very large contract that could secure funding for the organisation for the next three years.

Successful leaders must be able to communicate in different ways and in such a way as to reach their various audiences. This will almost certainly include learning to become technologically capable and able to use all sorts of programmes, including social media, in a way that engages and gets the message across. Many modern successful leaders have blogs, videos on YouTube and a plethora of followers on Twitter, and regularly communicate with many audiences in this way. I am a great fan of eating and drinking with staff in a social way, to give them the relaxed opportunity to share ideas. We call it a 'sounding board', where we discuss an idea over a meal, which encourages staff to relax and share their ideas. I have certainly learned a great deal from staff during this time. We also have 'wine time', again where staff can chat and mull over ideas in an informal setting. This is separate to celebration times, which are also very important and are often the result of us doing something that came from a great idea during a discussion. Good leaders thank their staff and praise them regularly and meaningfully. I am always surprised that those of us who work with children and place such value on praising and meaningfully celebrating children's contributions fail to do so with staff. It's a common criticism that so many staff don't feel valued and have to climb huge mountains to receive a little praise.

Great leaders stand back and give credit to their followers. Successful leaders not only behave in a particular way to guarantee success, they have certain leadership styles which they apply according to the situation. Getting the right style for the right situation seems to indicate a higher chance of success. Professor Carol Aubrey of Warwick University (2007) conducted an investigation using 12 case studies to examine the most suitable leadership styles for those in early childhood organisations. She found that there was no single style of adult leadership suitable for all types of early years provision. What she did find was that the most successful early childhood leaders were those who created a 'participative culture' and gave their staff the opportunity to exert 'bottom-up' influences on their own professional practice. She also noted that effective leadership involved adopting different forms of leadership in order to provide different services and to achieve greater clarity of professional roles, and very sensibly, she tells us that all models of early childhood leadership will be constrained by internal institutional factors and governmental or local authority regulations. Aubrey's leadership models are very humane and empower leaders by getting them to accept that certain behaviour is out of their control. This idea resonates with Cotter (2004), who referred to a 'zone of adaptability' where leaders can move out of their comfort zone and change their style but stay true to themselves so as to remain authentic and adaptable. He warned of a 'fake zone', where leaders forced themselves to adapt beyond their capabilities so they were no longer true to themselves and their adaptability was compromised at the expense of authenticity. Marilyn Manning and Patricia Haddock, communication and training consultants, summarise the main features of successful leaders. According to them, successful leaders commit themselves to their organisation and foster the same kind of commitment in their followers. They then ensure they:

- Know their job and field thoroughly
- Stay on top of current developments, trends and theories

- Know their people, including their strengths, weaknesses, hopes and goals
- Share a vision of service, excellence and achievement with others
- Demonstrate by their words and actions a strength of character.

(Manning and Haddock,1989, p. 11)

The emerging picture of a successful leader requires us to know a lot, understand a lot and operate within a complex and complicated world. It's not an easy role to step up to. Many leaders have identified the position as lonely, tiring, full of negative challenges and high expectations. It is therefore worth recalling what makes leaders *unsuccessful*. Poor leadership is defined by specific behaviour, which includes the following:

- No vision or sense of direction
- Failing to be accountable and take responsibility
- Poor knowledge and unwillingness to learn
- Not getting things done
- Failing to address conflicts and negative issues quickly enough
- Thinking that change is easy and will just happen through osmosis
- Insensitivity to staff, not knowing them and being unable to support their development
- Not questioning themselves
- Unwillingness to go the extra mile.

In light of what can go wrong, Shea's seven positive controls of good leadership (1990) are effective pointers:

- Control the execution of the mission
- Control the timing
- Control the people to make sure things are followed through
- Control the process of delegation down through the ranks
- Control the means of communication and information flow
- Control yourself.

(Shea,1990, p. 95)

Think and reflect!

Complete the following questionnaire and be honest with yourself. Reflect on why you have chosen to lead.

Consider doing one thing differently as a result of completing the questionnaire.

Do you think you are a successful leader?

This questionnaire has been completed by a hypothetical leader. Have a go at answering the questions in the first column yourself, and use the third column to assess your own leadership. Perhaps you could make an action plan to improve the areas that are weaker or missing.

Do you...?	Can you give an example?	Really?
Have a vision and direction that excites you and others?	I want to lead the first outstanding centre setting in the region.	I must check my staff team knows and see if I can list what excites them about this?
Show people what must happen to realise the vision?	Yes, there is an action plan up on the noticeboard in the office.	When did I last discuss this with the staff team?
Ensure everyone understands how they contribute to achieving the vision through team objectives?	Yes, all the departments have the vision as part of their annual development plan. I have agreed what needs doing and helped staff to see the connection.	I should ask the Finance and the Admin teams to articulate the vision and how they are helping to achieve it. I'll see if they can!
Approach the vision with passion, enthusiasm and confidence?	I sold the idea at a staff meeting by telling them how much we would benefit both as a setting and as individuals, including better training options, reduced paperwork and more secure funding; all the things that are currently worrying us as a staff team.	I have been checking that others have responded positively to the vision by having informal conversations with each staff member.
Mobilise the staff's enthusiasm, curiosity, energy and talents?	I use 'thank you' cards, celebrations and photo displays, all showing steps towards outstanding practice.	I should consider extra ways to maintain enthusiasm, for example, by having a staff team 'big treat'.
Make things happen that you and the staff care about?	I secured funding for the outdoor project, which staff all agreed would be a step forward.	Yes, we even have trained two staff on Forest School so we could really extend our outdoor fun.
Show an interest in the staff and show you care?	I use congratulations cards, birthday treats and try hard to remember personal information, even things such as whose daughter has just passed her piano test.	Well, I suppose I could be better. I will review my system for remembering special dates.

Managing changes

Do you...?	Can you give an example?	Really?
Lead change with confidence and intelligence?	*I have introduced regular emails and an information board, which have clear statements about what is happening and news updates to ensure the information about changes is available. I also include thank yous to staff who have been helping the process.*	*Am I sure everyone knows? I must ask the cleaner!*
Take time to be sensitive to how others might feel and act accordingly?	*I arranged a time to take the new staff out for lunch to help settle their anxieties, which I picked up on in a random conversation with a few members of staff. I will try and build in a lunch with me as part of the induction. It's worth the price of a pizza to help new staff start on a positive footing.*	*Actually, I got very irritated at the staff meeting by what seemed like whinging. It's not my choice to make the change. It's the government agenda!*
Talk and listen to your staff?	*I sent an email to the two nurseries containing times for them to call me to discuss the latest changes, as I am off-site a lot.*	*I texted them my mobile number and said I was very happy to get feedback face to face or by phone, email or text. It's worked well with the young staff.*
Give the staff a space to share their ideas and expectations?	*I arranged cover for each team to have an hour to look at what they need and want to do as a team. Set up a whiteboard where they wrote their ideas.*	*Having time together was a good idea, so I have agreed to do this again for the next few weeks while the team formulate their plan. As we progress I will build in an hour of cover to give the team the chance to take stock and update a section of the information board.*
React constructively to all types of conflict and aim for harmony?	*This is hard work as I have little time for whingers. I have pre-empted most of this by giving the biggest whinger the chance to lead the process and setting her the task of helping her colleagues bring it alive.*	*It's very trying at times to keep positive. I just want to shout and say, 'Just get on with the job, I am not asking you to climb to base camp Everest in your slippers. Just make the setting better for the children!'*
Support your team's development?	*I arranged a fun away day with the Circus Company. Lots of laughter and chat: it was very positive.*	*It's true, I even did the trapeze.*

Teamwork

Do you...?	Can you give an example?	Really?
Give the team autonomy in decision-making and make them accountable for the results they achieve?	*Each group was allocated £100 to use to turn their improvement plan into action. The teams made their plans and executed them their way. I stood right back.*	*Now we some fabulous song boxes, outdoor activity boxes, and sensory walls. The staff are very proud, as am I. The parents loved the changes And the children delighted.*
Make sure the team can act effectively in your absence?	*I have developed an 'operations handbook' with all the policies and procedures in alphabetical order and linked to the welfare standards.*	*No crises or complaints yet.*
Emotionally connect to your team?	*Again, it's the little things that show I care. I text personal greetings, phone if they look sad or worried, and if possible I take a positive interest in their home lives. I try and pick up little treats such as walnut whirls and favourite biscuits to show I am thinking about them and understand their state of mind.*	*It can be tricky to get this right as I don't want to seem patronising or intrusive. I try to be friendly rather than friends, where possible. I have to remember fairness and balance so it doesn't look like one person is favoured over another.*
Make the staff feel valued and celebrate with them?	*Praise, thanks and rewards are my favourites. Annual treats such as a visit to the greyhound races, getting the nursery picture in the local paper when staff have done something they are delighted with, a mention in Nursery World, a picture on the website, getting the staff involved in a wider project or including them in some research has been very motivating also. In summary, anything that says I am proud of my team, what they do and how they do it.*	*Keeping the website updated with success stories and also contacting the local press has been good marketing and PR for us.*
Give credit where credit is due and take the flak?	*I am very conscious about ensuring praise goes to where it is due and that people who deserve it receive it. My job is to enjoy the good times but take it on the chin when things go wrong. There is nothing worse than the leader who takes all the credit when things go well and blames their team when things are difficult.*	*It can be difficult sometimes to give praise and credit without sounding cheesy, but I try to find something meaningful to say as much as possible. It is worth the effort.*
Share an interest in what staff hold important?	*The children; there is nothing that impresses more than when I talk to the staff about individual children in a way that shows I notice what they do and how they have supported a child's development.*	*I have to work very hard to get to know all the children and recognise their foibles and ways so I can add to the discussion, rather than just coming into the class and patting a head.*

Personal development

Do you...?	Can you give an example?	Really?
Continue to learn and develop your own knowledge?	*I am doing the National Professional Qualification in Integrated Centre Leadership (NPQICL) award.*	*Yes, really! I read Nursery World on the bus to work, use the National Strategies Website and read research papers.*
Keep a close eye on standards and quality?	*I insist that staff read relevant information. Points to note and relevant details are published in a weekly information sheet. I have joined the National Day Nursery Association to get their briefings. I need to attend and enable staff to attend the local professional cluster meetings more often.*	*OK, maybe I could do better monitoring. It is hard to always be checking and rechecking in the busy day. It's true how easy it is to assume people are doing what you ask.*
Make sure that all working conditions are appropriate?	*I make regular checks around the setting, but I think I could do more on this.*	*I should take a 'temperature check' by asking staff some simple questions.*
Go the extra mile?	*Yes, I come in on occasional weekends when I want to get something sorted. I will stay late without worrying. I get things for nursery when on holiday. Took Freddie the Bear on holiday and had photo taken on the beach with him.*	*I did and I gave up space for a pair of shoes in my suitcase to make room for Freddie!*

2 Leadership know-how

Although the concept of leadership has been a subject of speculation for a very long time, it was not the subject of scientific research until the twentieth century. Researchers tended to define leadership according to their own points of view and the elements that most interested them, thus influencing the investigation and analysis. The one thing they did appear to agree on was that the definition was arbitrary and some definitions were more useful than others, but ultimately there was no single correct definition. After a comprehensive review of the leadership literature, Stogdill (1974) concluded that 'there are almost as many definitions of leadership as there are persons who have attempted to define the concept' (Stogdill, 1974, p. 259).

In the past, leadership in early years received scant attention and what research was done was led by a select group of researchers. The sector is quite complex including statutory, private and voluntary services which all have different issues in terms of leadership and management and so a one-hat-fits-all approach was impossible and probably limited the research. However, there has been more research recently, not least because early years came under the government's radar, and has been the focus of attention, policy development and extensive change since 2004, when the then Government wrote the National Childcare Strategy. That said, it is worth noting that much of this research reflects school leadership, despite the increasing numbers of nursery settings.

Since then there has been a raft of Government legislation and policy initiatives to drive the strategy. It took a while before serious questions were asked as to who would put all these changes into place and the issue of leadership came into focus. Let me give you a round-up of the changes that have occurred during the last twenty years.

Over the past twenty years, early years legislation has focused on following three policy drivers:

1   Childcare to enable families to work, especially women

2   High quality early years education to help narrow the gap and increase the educational success of children from poor and disadvantaged families

3   Early intervention and support for families.

A quick round-up shows the pace of change. Starting in 1998 with the National Literacy strategy, this was followed in 1999 with the SureStart trailblazer of 60 settings, with a plan for 250 by 2002. Then, in 2000, the Early Learning Goals replaced the Desirable Outcomes and the QCA Curriculum Guidance for the Foundation Stage. In 2001, the Special Educational Needs Code of Practice came into force, and the National Standards for Under 8s Day Care and Child-minding. By 2002, the Birth to Three Matters and the Neighbourhood Nursery Initiative were underway. In 2003 came the Every Child Matters Consultation on Government plans to reform children's services, in response to Victoria Climbie's death. This became law in 2004, which was also the year of Early Support and the Foundation Stage profile as well as the EPPE Final Report. The Education Act was also amended to align early years inspections with school inspections. In 2005, the CWDC was formed to lead workforce issues that needed to be addressed in order to ensure legislation and policy would be implemented. In 2006, the Childcare Act introduced the Ofsted Childcare Register with the proposal that a graduate should lead every setting and that staff should be Level 3 qualified. The Act gave children's centres a specific statutory basis, and placed new duties on local authorities to establish and maintain sufficient childcare places to meet local needs. This was the Act that pushed the free entitlement policy through, originally with 12.5 free hours and then with 15. In 2007 the Every Parent Matters strategy was produced as well as the Letters and Sounds Pack to aid the teaching of phonics. That was also the year of the Primary National Strategy, the Graduate Leaders Fund and Every Child a Reader, Every Child a Writer and Every Child Counts support programmes. In 2008, the EYFS became mandatory, including welfare requirements and statutory adult-to-child ratios. In 2009 Every Child a Talker (ECAT) came into being in recognition that the richness of language could make a significant difference to a child's long-term success in school. This was the year when health published their Healthy Child programme, which looked at ways to better support parents, especially those most vulnerable.

With the arrival of the Coalition Government, the sector was keen for things to slow down so the strategies could be fully embedded. The comprehensive spending review in October 2010 was used to review and slim down policy excess. The free funding for three and four year olds was protected and there was a promise to increase health visitors and provide 15 hours free childcare for the 20% of most disadvantaged two year olds, increasing it to 40% by September 2014. The Government was supportive of the work done by Graham Allen and Frank Field about the impact of early intervention, and the Early Intervention Foundation was also established to develop and help roll out more evidence-based services to families.

In 2012, the Government published their vision of an integrated service via Supporting Families in the Foundation Years report. This was followed by the Nutbrown Review, which examined the best way to shape and improve the status and qualifications of the workforce in order to support quality education. In 2013 the More Affordable Childcare scheme was implemented, with an additional £200m support in the form of universal credit for poorer families, the EY premium, and the plan to introduce a tax-free childcare scheme worth up to 20% of childcare fees by Autumn 2015.

However, the 2013 report More Great Childcare produced some unpopular polices, including:

- Child-minding agencies
- The introduction of the EY teacher role which does not have Qualified Teacher Status

- Removal of local authorities' duty to support, advise and train those running good settings
- The duty of local authorities to support only those settings which require improvement or are inadequate
- Changes to funding criteria (based on Ofsted criteria only)
- The introduction of baseline assessments from Reception
- Free early education for two year olds in school.

Over the last twenty years, we can see how early years staff across the sectors have had to show how they would provide strong foundations for all children in their care, including refocusing the way they supported parents, extending preventative services for vulnerable children and those identified as being 'at risk', and creating seamless services where multi-agencies would work collaboratively to benefit local families. Given this, it is not surprising that effective and knowledgeable leadership remains critical to the success of an organisation, and particularly where the focus of the work is on those children from poor and disadvantaged homes. Competent and plausible leadership has a powerful influence, not just on the effectiveness of children's services but, more importantly, on the learning experiences of children. According to Muijis et al. (2004), leadership that is committed, competent and respected is one of the main distinguishing factors between the most and least successful children centre programmes. Unsuccessful programmes are characterised by less experienced leadership; that is, leaders who are less skilled at training and supervising staff, less good at working with schools and the community, and less involved and committed.

It has been shown that how leaders support their staff, provide intellectual stimulation for them and create an organisational culture is also critical to the success of children's learning and development. Leaders who recognise the need to motivate, negotiate, influence staff and create teams which share the vision leads to higher staff retention, which is extremely beneficial to those using the organisation and to the community in which they are based.

Leadership characteristics

Back in the 1990s, Jillian Rodd began to identify early years leadership characteristics and found a lack of agreement within the sector about the abilities and competencies necessary to lead. She warned that the consequence of failing to agree a concept of leadership could result in difficulties for leaders who would need to have a set of skills and knowledge to enable them to respond effectively in the fast-changing sector where leaders increasingly needed to be entrepreneurial in order to develop the service. She saw the importance of and the need to 'build, establish and maintain professional credibility with those who use early childhood services' (Rodd, 1997, p. 40).

The concept of leadership characteristics had already been explored in other sectors and was generally considered to be a means of grouping concepts and ideas together under a more general category. This usually included the following:

- Abilities and skills
- Industry-based knowledge
- Personal values
- Relationships
- Reputation and track record.

Kets de Vries's (2001) study of leadership characteristics found that there were three characteristics which continually received more than 50% of the votes in every study across the globe. These were: honesty, inspiration and competence.

As Rodd (1996) explored leadership in the early years, she developed a set of characteristics needed for this particular area of leadership. She identified personal characteristics such as being warm, kind, nurturing, patient and friendly as important for leading an early years setting. I think she was right, as these are still very important characteristics. Whether they are the crucial ones is subject to further debate. She identified staff as needing to have professional competence and the ability to act as both a guide and mentor. She saw leaders as accountable for a quality service. She tried to link some of these characteristics to specific tasks, which was probably a bit simplistic for today's more complex early years leaders' role. For example, she linked being rational, logical and analytical to the professional skills needed to manage finance and for the leadership role to train and develop staff. Certainly Rodd's work contributed to a debate that was necessary in order to identify what the leaders of the fast-changing world of early childhood would need to be able to do to make a real difference.

Six years later, Ebbeck and Waniganayake (2002) were still concerned that there was no set of agreed common expectations for leaders in early years and no real examples of successful leaders to point to. This is not to say the debate had stopped. In fact there was growing agreement that leadership was a critical factor for successful children's services; but the sector was still quite modest and had not quite captured the attention of policy makers, who today put childcare at the centre of economic and social policies.

However, in 2000, the National College for School Leadership (NCSL) was formed, and began to establish a common understanding of the distinctive and different abilities required by leaders and managers of children's services. This developed into the Championing Children framework of 2006.

Championing Children is a framework that establishes a shared set of skills, knowledge and behaviours for those who lead and manage integrated children's services. It provides a common understanding about the particular abilities required by leaders and managers of these services.

Individuals, teams and organisations can use this document as a planning tool to help develop the skills, knowledge and behaviours necessary.

(Championing Children, 2006, p. 1)

The National Standards of the NCSL were developed to be both aspirational and inspirational, reflecting the excitement, complexity and challenge of the role of the leader of a setting. The Standards set out the role of leadership in a series of expectations, including how the leader creates the right environment in terms of vision and direction and how that vision is translated into an inclusive, integrated and responsive service and environment that supports children to learn and flourish, and makes parents feel welcome and able to engage. An emphasis was placed on collaboration with other services and the whole of the community. Leaders were expected to understand the concept of continuous improvement and how that is translated into a core operating principle. These expectations are still held to be valid for early years leaders.

The National Standards are grouped into six key areas, each of which are broken down into the professional knowledge and professional quality and skills needed to demonstrate competence. All areas are interdependent and are of equal importance.

The six key areas are:

- Leading Learning and Development
- Shaping the Present and Creating the Future
- Building and Strengthening Teams, Stronger Families, Stronger Communities
- Managing the Organisation
- Being Accountable and Responsible
- Improved Outcomes for Children and Families.

Championing Children 2006 highlighted seven aspects of management and/or leadership, all but one of which map directly onto either the NHS Leadership and Management Standards or the Common Core for the frontline Children's Workforce.

The seven aspects of management and/or leadership are:

- Achieving outcomes
- Safeguarding and promoting the welfare of children
- Providing direction
- Leading and managing change
- Working with people
- Managing information
- Communicating and engaging effectively with children, young people and families.

At the London Early Years Foundation, a childcare social enterprise where I have worked for over ten years, a simpler model was developed to highlight the significant elements of the role of a nursery leader.

The London Early Years Foundation leadership framework

Putting frameworks into practice

It should not come as a surprise to anyone that the leader of a setting must lead and manage the organisation and be accountable to all those who use the services, those who work within it, those who fund it and those who govern it. The leader is responsible for the quality of the work, for the staff and for the finance and business management. They are expected to create organisational structures that support the effective delivery of services and lead the organisation forward with relevant processes in place that comply with legal requirements. Leadership covers a wide range of responsibilities from robust financial management to ensuring a pedagogy that is underpinned by best practice. While doing all of this, the leader needs to remember to sustain and demonstrate personal motivation and to inspire and support all staff, especially during periods of change. As anyone in a leadership role knows, building teams, sustaining them and supporting staff personal development can bring great joy but can also be extremely hard work.

However, unlike generic leadership competence and characteristics, there are criteria that are specific to the principles of safeguarding the child's welfare and supporting children's learning which require particular professional knowledge and skill. For example, in order to be able to review and evaluate learning, teaching and care practice and to identify, promote and encourage effective practice in order to promote improvement in outcomes for children and families, you would need to know how children develop and learn as well as understanding how this is applied within the national frameworks. In the early years sector this would include the EYFS framework. To ensure both these things align, you would also be expected to know and understand the principles of what constitutes effective observation, learning, teaching and assessment and how you would apply this to create a learning culture for children, staff and parents. The qualities and skills needed to translate this into operational practice would include having enthusiasm and commitment to learning, being able to help parents engage in their children's learning, and an ability to use monitoring data to improve the service.

Another area which may be new for many leaders in the sector is to have a comprehensive understanding of their local community and its strengths and be able to develop the capacity of community organisations and individuals to support sustainable community development. In the past, some leaders had these skills and this knowledge because they had a personal interest, especially managers of community nurseries. However, having an ability to understand and connect with the local community remains quite a challenge as these are a distinct set of skills, especially when early years leaders are expected to raise educational expectations and aspirations within the communities for all families. Leaders of many settings are, through the Children's Centre agenda, expected to ensure effective distribution of information using a wide range of media. This is quite a task for many as it requires a new set of skills and attitudes and a willingness to use imaginative opportunities, not least finding the time and skill to network in order to include the wider community and seeking and using feedback to improve and shape services.

The challenges of negotiating and mediating both with and between those individuals and groups to break down barriers and promote better mutual understanding is not to be underestimated. The interesting test is how leaders benchmark their own behaviour and knowledge against their own and others' perception of effective leadership.

This is also a challenge for those who manage leaders, for example trustees, governors and heads of services, as they try to measure the impact of their subordinates in terms of how they make a difference.

Examples of leadership characteristics

Leadership characteristics have developed apace and there are now a number of models. Moyles et al. (2007) developed a system called the Effective Leadership and Management Scheme for the early years (ELMS). This was conceptualised as an elm tree and described the qualities, skills, attributes, characteristics and attitudes necessary for effective leadership. I like the metaphor of a tree and the images of a strong trunk symbolising growth, strength and reliability, and the branches leading and opening and representing the greater detail of:

1. Leadership qualities

2. Management skills

3. Professional skills and attributes

4. Personal characteristics and attitudes.

> *These four branches were identified through the research as being the key areas that constitute effective early years leadership and management. They encompass all the essential components necessary for effective leadership and management which appear within at least one of the branches. On the branches are subsections called 'stems': these are the embedded qualities, skills, attributes, characteristics and attitudes that grow out of the four main branches. Each stem has further subsections called 'leaves'. These reflect more defined, precise qualities, skills, attributes, characteristics and attitudes required of effective leaders and managers.*
>
> (Moyles, 2007, p. 12–13)

Moyles' system was built from the principle of self-reflection, which can create a climate where thinking is encouraged and intelligent self-questioning, although painful and disconcerting at times, can lead to greater development of the individual and the service. It is a view shared by Fullan (2003), who wrote fluently on the role of leadership and who considered active reflection as the best route to discover and rediscover the ways that leaders understand themselves and their role, and how this translates into reality; and, most importantly, whether the impact is positive or negative.

Moyles (2007) captured some of the anxiety about leadership when she noted that there is an inclination to see leadership characteristics in people of heroic abilities. What she said she wanted was to develop:

> *[s]uccessful leaders who do not learn to 'do' leadership and then stick to set patterns and ways of doing things along a prescribed set of known rules [. . . but] are willing to change in response to new sets of circumstances – and to the different needs of children . . . and teachers.*
>
> (Riley and MacBeth, 2003, p. 174; quoted in Moyles, 2007, p. 19)

In order to lead, I believe you need to balance pragmatism with compromise. This is something which I feel leads to a humane and intelligent management and a motivated and engaged staff. Sadly, it is often lacking in many settings, particularly when considering how to apply statutory requirements. Health and safety is often where this is tested and here the experienced, confident and well-informed leader can be the one to make the difference by applying common sense and compromise rather than trying to apply the letter of the law, which is often inappropriate in reality.

Leaders need to understand the business so as to make the vision real. Our business is the world of the child and how we help children achieve their potential in a lively, appropriate and fun way. We need to kindle a lifelong capacity and excitement for learning in them. We also need to be able to understand and form reciprocal relationships with parents and inspire them to become lifelong champions of learning themselves.

Some people expect leaders to be charismatic. I think this is a challenge, as so many people in leadership positions are there because they have gone through the ranks and arrived at the top through the hierarchical journey. While this can produce some great leaders, it can just as likely produce people who are neither creative nor courageous thinkers but know how to keep a solid service on the road. This is satisfactory only if they can make a long-term difference to children and the sector as a whole. What leaders definitely need to be is credible, able to command respect by behaving with confidence and integrity, and able to communicate so as to tell the story of what is happening or needs to happen in a way that supports staff, engages them and secures their loyalty.

Aubrey (2007) also examined leadership qualities through her study with early years leaders, and identified a range of 'categories for effective leadership practice':

- Identifying and articulating a collective vision
- Ensuring shared understandings, meanings and goals
- Effective communication
- Encouraging reflection
- Monitoring and assessing practice
- Committing to ongoing, professional development
- Distributing leadership
- Building a learning community and team culture
- Encouraging and facilitating parent and community partnership
- Leading amid managing: striking the balance.

(Aubrey, 2007, p. 12)

So far, all early years research implies a certain agreement as to the characteristics necessary to lead in early years. However, this work can be augmented by the concept of leadership competence created mostly within the workplace.

Leadership competencies

A competency is a description of the behaviour or actions needed to perform a particular aspect of a role at work. Each role requires a number of competencies and most people learn new competencies as they progress in their job role as it changes with time.

The purpose of a competence-based workforce is to help individuals to consistently perform work activities to the standards required in employment, over a range of contexts or conditions. Job descriptions tell someone the main things they are responsible for, while competencies set out the behaviour and actions needed to carry out those responsibilities effectively and in line with the organisational values. Competencies are linked to evidence of the outcomes achieved.

Understandably, many organisations are keen on this particular approach, especially as the competency framework gives clear indicators of what is expected of their leaders. This helps them manage and evaluate staff performance more clearly and is a useful tool in developing recruitment, induction and staff development programmes.

The competencies model has also found favour with many local authorities, and there are some interesting examples. Some local authorities have chosen competences which they consider will underpin success by being relevant to many roles. For example:

- Adaptability
- Business initiative
- Innovative thinking
- Interpersonal skills
- Leadership
- Organisation awareness
- Planning and organising
- Problem-solving
- Professional expertise
- Service focus
- Working in partnership.

These local authorities work from the principle that the competencies are better if they are flexible and used to support systems such as:

- Recruiting and selecting
- Managing and reviewing people's performance
- Training and development
- Building teams and organisations
- Succession planning and managing careers.

In that way, the competencies provide a framework for the local authority to adapt more easily and readily to the changing world and prepare staff to meet the challenges of greater commercialism, diversity, new legislation, technology and different ways of working with colleagues.

Other organisations use competency clusters such as a 'drive' cluster with a focus on excellent service through business initiative, planning and organising. Another example is a 'reasoning' cluster, which emphasises problem-solving, innovative thinking, professional expertise and organisational awareness. Outside London, some counties have developed a competency matrix with an emphasis on distributed leadership. They use it as a tool for planning, performance management and job descriptions as well as as an audit to examine strengths and weaknesses. Headings, while differently written, are inherently covering similar ground and common features including:

- Vision
- Chaos management and managing complexity
- Guardianship and accountability
- Emotional intelligence, valuing self and others
- Change facilitation
- Securing benefits for children and young people.

The approach is that each leader, whether in governance or operations, uses the matrix to understand what is expected of them. Competencies can throw up conundrums, especially on the issue of what is leadership and how it differs from management, but this can also be the basis of a healthy and informative debate.

Adair (2002) and Moyles (2007) rated the ability to develop and communicate a clear vision that sets challenging standards and objectives and inspires staff to achieve excellence in line with organisational strategy. They also picked up on the theme of culture setting, which requires leaders to be able to translate the vision into achievable targets for each nursery in such a way that staff want to achieve them. They then expanded this further by compelling leaders to be genuinely enthusiastic about delivering the vision and creating systems that enable this to happen at every level. They also believed that leaders consider role-modelling a means of setting standards. Aubrey's (2007) research found that leaders stress the importance of leading the provision of quality care, raising achievement and staff performance with an emphasis on coaching, mentoring and staff development. Children's achievement was also considered a critical factor. But she did warn that there appeared to be little evidence of the analysis of characteristics against effectiveness measures. Competencies may be easier to measure as they are linked to job descriptions and, as many focus on relationships issues such as complaints, could be more easily evidenced.

Finally, there is generally a shared view that leaders create the values, standards and expectations of the organisation and then persuade and influence the staff to accept and apply them in order to achieve the organisational vision and purpose. In the early years, this includes having a clear vision both in terms of organisational development and also, and most importantly, in terms of a shared pedagogy. Leaders in the early years therefore need to have competencies in a whole range of areas so they can create an organisation that weaves together all the critical elements of leadership in order to make a positive difference at every level of the service, and for the future of children, staff and the early years sector. It is some task!

Think and reflect!

When did you last assess your leadership in action?

The questionnaire below has been completed by a hypothetical leader. Have a go at answering the questions yourself and use the answers to assess your own leadership. Afterwards, try making an action plan to improve the areas that were exposed as weaker or missing.

Management tasks

Do I...?	Is it a regular task?	What skills and knowledge do I need to do this?	What makes this a leadership task?
Set annual targets for the setting?	Yes, I have used the Self-Evaluation Form (SEF) as the basis for identifying areas for improvement, and then recorded the targets on the annual development plan.	I need to better understand what the staff and I define as good practice, link it to the research on quality, and then identify what areas of weakness we have and how to write analytically rather than just stating the obvious.	It helps me set out the direction for the year. It means I can set the tone of the organisation more easily and turn this into real practice so staff can see what they are being judged against. It means I have a better grasp of what training and improvements are needed so I can develop my budget more accurately.
Attend management meetings?	Yes	I need to better prepare for the meeting so I can participate more effectively. When I chair I need to manage the agenda and ensure we have a focused meeting with clear actions, not just a noisy talking shop!	As the leader I am expected to ensure the right items are discussed so we can progress and also use the meeting to check staff understanding and pick up areas which will need further action.

Do I . . .?	Is it a regular task?	What skills and knowledge do I need to do this?	What makes this a leadership task?
Develop policies and procedures?	Yes, both as initiator and part of a working group.	I need to be alert to legal changes and practice expectations and then be quicker to amend policies so our practice is updated in line with the new changes.	Policies are part of the infrastructure needed to be in place to ensure the setting is operating within the ethos I, as the leader, set out.
Lead the staff meeting and listen and respond to their ideas?	Yes, although it is a shared agenda and staff have the opportunity to add items for discussion (within a certain time frame).	I try hard to listen and empathise with staff and create a space where staff feel able to discuss all sorts of issues from new policies to managing other staff. Creating a warm and open space for discussion also has a risk as staff are more able to challenge and this means they can ruffle colleagues' feathers and feelings may run high. While I need to understand staff tensions, I also need to be able to manage the meeting so that it ends constructively.	I have stopped 'any other business' (AOB) at meetings because staff have been using this to bring up quite complex issues at the end of the meeting, with little chance to fully address them and resulting in them adding to conflict. I am trying to get everyone to the point where they can understand the importance of adding an agenda item in partnership with the chair, so we can plan enough time into the meeting for a useful debate that leads to a positive solution. It also gives me a head start in understanding the point of conflict so I understand the issues fully before it comes to a larger meeting.
Lead responsibility for health and safety?	Yes. I have also delegated it to every staff member; they have all learned that health and safety is not just about the children, families, visitors, students,	I am always trying to keep up to speed with the issues of compliance. My way of doing this is to constantly read magazines and briefings. I need to be able to coach staff on health and safety on a daily basis and ensure they have the right training, such as	As a leader I have to ensure balance between what are relevant and good play experiences against perceived dangers. I have to set the standard as staff panic and will be quick to cancel or stop activities. I have to ensure a critical review

Do I . . .?	Is it a regular task?	What skills and knowledge do I need to do this?	What makes this a leadership task?
	etc., but that staff also have a duty of care to themselves and their colleagues and need to be mindful of this at every stage of their work.	risk assessment, manual handling, Control of Substances Hazardous to Health (COSSH), etc. I need to ensure we have regular health and safety meetings which are minuted and create an environment where everyone knows their duty of care to the children, staff, themselves and the organisation. When it comes to health and safety I must make it a 'we' approach with a shared sense of responsibility.	is undertaken after any health and safety breach or accident so we can address the issue sensibly and learn from it.
Set up learning activities?	No, although I check the quality of what is happening with the children by looking at the planning, asking staff questions about it and observing.	Understanding my role as a pedagogical leader is critical here because my job is to ensure the children are getting the best learning opportunities. If I don't know how to do that, then the chances of it happening consistently are limited. I must therefore ensure the children have a good routine, environment, competent staff and learning opportunities. I need to create a philosophy which gets the whole staff team working together to continually create experiences that are relevant, stimulating and fun for children.	It is all about ethos and ensuring this is evident at every level of the service. It's also about picking up strengths and weaknesses and being able to lead either through modelling and discussion, one to one with staff, or creating training and programmes that strengthen knowledge and practice in specific areas.
Work directly with the children?	Sometimes, but not as often as I would like.	I must use all my knowledge of child development, how children learn and what makes an enriched curriculum and the basis	This is important, because it demonstrates to staff that you understand what you are leading and that you are very interested in

Do I . . .?	Is it a regular task?	What skills and knowledge do I need to do this?	What makes this a leadership task?
		of this. I must also have a means of measuring quality such as Early Childhood Environment Rating scales R and E and levels of engagement.	what they do. It also informs discussions about children and families.
Sort lunch and sit and eat with the children?	Sometimes, when short-staffed I will sort lunch. I often eat with the children to sample food and be visible.	I have had to really improve my knowledge of what constitutes good nutrition and the menus we use. I am obsessed with providing seasonal dishes, and home baking. We now have 'Fish Fridays'. Lunch is a very important and formal time, where children all eat together, learn to use cutlery and serve themselves. I insist on napkins and ask staff to sit with the children and eat with them. The older children have a table on their own as if they were in a restaurant.	Leading from the front has to mean that staff know I am always alert to what is happening and willing to step in when needed but not take over.
Complete children's observations?	No, I oversee and monitor them.	I have revised learning journeys. I am using information from cohort tracking to set a baseline for each child and then collect evidence of their improvement against the baseline information. Staff are learning to include their assessment and development targets so parents and children can follow their learning journey. My challenge is to help staff link the children's development more effectively to planning	Keeping a grasp of the main means of ensuring the curriculum is good enough. This is particularly critical where children are fully dependent on staff to provide the first steps to education. As the leader, monitoring is a means of assessing whether the setting is making a difference, narrowing the gap between educational failure and success or ensuring the children and their families are getting the best service.

Do I . . .?	Is it a regular task?	What skills and knowledge do I need to do this?	What makes this a leadership task?
		and ensure differentiated activities are also part of the process to support and extend the children's abilities. I need to monitor our system of parental input and ensure we are having children's planning meetings as part of the process.	
Support staff with children's challenges?	Absolutely.	New safeguarding behaviour management policies are in place for two year olds to ensure staff know what to do if they believe a child needs more protection. I need constantly to offer training and support. I have also introduced Makaton as a means of reducing some tantrums from children frustrated by their inability to communicate.	I never leave staff to struggle. I know that leaders who are never there when staff need support are abdicating their duties and will never earn the respect of staff.

Organisational responsibilities

Do I . . .?	Is it a regular task?	What skills and knowledge do I need to do this?	What makes this a leadership task?
Complete accident forms?	If appropriate, but I certainly check the six monthly monitoring.	I have rewritten our forms to include all the necessary information needed to be collected so as to limit us failing to get an answer to all the critical issues when staff are stressed having just dealt with an accident. I have learned through experience that staff need to be trained to complete the forms properly.	This is part of the health and safety responsibility.
Complete an Individual Education Plan (IEP)?	I rarely do this as I have a SENCO in each nursery. However, if I was without a SENCO then I might have to seek support from the local authority Inclusion Manager who helps train the staff about IEPs.	I have read the Special Education Needs Code of Practice and used this as the basis of the SEN policy. I have sought the help of the local authority to ensure the staff are able to agree suitable targets and know how and when to involve parents in the process.	This is not in itself a leadership task, but I need to be able to lead at all times,, or delegate appropriately or get advice if I am not sure of something. It is imperative that I show I am continually learning and keeping up to speed with what makes the best service for children.
Arrange a review meeting for a child funded by Local Authority Children's Services?	Again, as needed. I know that some places have delegated staff but in other places the manager is the lead.	I need to understand the process and local authority procedures including funding criteria. Once we have a child who is funded by the local authority I have to know what they want from me in terms of parental involvement, assessment of the child's progress and any other criteria against which they will be monitoring.	As the leader, I must know the external means of supporting children, families and staff. This means being able to access funds, negotiate contracts and ensure compliance against contracted responsibilities.

Do I . . .?	Is it a regular task?	What skills and knowledge do I need to do this?	What makes this a leadership task?
Sort out the staffing rotas for the week?	No, we have an administrator who does this.	I need to understand the process because I keep an eye on agency costs. I am also interested in monitoring changes in patterns of attendance so I can see what parents are looking for and may need to address this across the organisation. Clearly, I need to understand ratio requirements.	This process is not a leadership role necessarily, but having a system in place is. In addition, I find analysing trends and changing accordingly .is good practice.
Answer emails and telephone calls?	Yes, although not exclusively. I have limited opening emails to twice a day unless I am expecting an urgent one.	I have taken some time to become as technologically adept as my young staff. I am learning how to send group texts and emails to parents, especially in emergency situations such as having to close the nursery because of bad weather.	Having a system is important but not really a leadership task. As the leader, I am responsible for ensuring a policy is in place that covers communication, and that I keep abreast of issues that affect the organization, such as breaches of data protection through inappropriate use of social networking sites.
Have complete headcount details for a Nursery Education Grant?	I am lucky to have an administrator to do this as we have large number of children.	I understand the process, especially the headcount. I don't know the details of each child. I know what it represents in costs and income and what this means in terms of running our nursery.	We need to have a process in place to ensure that headcount happens, as it constitutes a large amount of our income. I am, however, leading the process of getting the funding increased in line with schools. It's my job to ensure we are represented at the Schools Forum.

Do I . . .?	Is it a regular task?	What skills and knowledge do I need to do this?	What makes this a leadership task?
Reconcile petty cash?	I have trained the deputy and two senior staff to do this but I check it randomly.	To do this I need finance skills and to know how to check it is happening so there is a clean financial audit.	Leadership is about going out and getting the money, rather than reconciling the petty cash. However, as a good leader, I have a secure and robust financial monitoring system in place.
Do the banking?	Sometimes, but trying to reduce this by getting more and more fees paid through BACS and via debit cards.	I need to have finance procedures and a good relationship with the bank. It's also worth considering investment and what I should do with any spare cash to gain some interest before it goes back out to pay the bills. Debt is a growing issue and our organisation, like it or not, has to give some consideration to managing parental debt.	I am setting up the system. As funds are mostly through fees, I need to understand everything otherwise there will be a risk of a deficit.
Check the budget and sort new invoices?	If possible I delegate, as it is best managed by the people responsible for the invoices. Big settings may have a finance officer.	I need to understand finance procedures and know how to set and manage a budget and link the budget to strategy.	I draft the budget in line with the strategy of the organisation and in the context of available funds. The budget is a critical process.
Complete the application form for capital funds for two-year-olds?	Yes, although I seek help from my governors.	I have to do this more and more and have learned how to read the questions in ways that ensure I give the right information.	Funding is one of my key roles as the leader, in particular finding out about funds, networking to get linked into funding opportunities and attending relevant

Do I . . . ?	Is it a regular task?	What skills and knowledge do I need to do this?	What makes this a leadership task?
			meetings to pick up useful leads and ideas. I've found it useful to partner up with another organisation to get a shared bid organised. I always need to have my 'ears close to the ground' and to be looking for ways of bringing money into the organisation to sustain and improve it.
Complete the resource audit and order new equipment?	No, I delegate this and ensure it is linked to annual plans.	I have written a procurement policy which covers where to purchase from, aligned with the organisation's values, e.g. local providers, fairtrade options, organic milk, etc.	This isn't part of my role as a leader. I've trained my manager and senior staff.
Plan a new display and delegate accordingly?	Sometimes, when it's part of a new plan.	I need to understand displays as a means of communicating.	As a leader, I have to ensure the values and ethos of my organisation are represented correctly and appropriately in public.
Prepare and attend monitoring meetings?	Yes, although I may delegate this.	I must be alert to the contract monitoring criteria, including expectations. I like to see the agenda in advance so I can prepare and I always read the action points from the previous meeting so I have done what I said I would and give a good impression at the meeting. Contractors need to feel I am taking them seriously.	If the meeting is important then I make sure I am free to attend, especially if I need to support staff or make strategic decisions.

Dealing with parents

Do I . . .?	Is it a regular task?	What skills and knowledge do I need to do this?	What makes this a leadership task?
Welcome and chat to parents?	Absolutely, but it is also the task of the staff who have a more intimate relationship with parents.	I need to be fully knowledgeable about the psychology of parenthood, the research about parental involvement and the best ways of communicating with parents.	A friendly warm welcome sets the scene, and it is important that I am part of this.
Take fees?	I don't take fees but I know in small settings it is often the job of the leader.	I need to know about methods of fee collection, inance procedures and debt management.	As the leader, it is about knowing the process, as fees are a main source of income and therefore needs a robust system from beginning to end, including fee setting and fee increases.
Meet new parents and show them around?	Yes, but it is not just me: every staff member is trained to be able to do this or is learning how to do this.	I need to be consistent in the information I give out, in person and over the telephone. It is not just enough to be friendly: parents need answers to particular questions. I need to ensure all staff are regularly trained – as well as myself. I also need to know about the various ways parents want to access nurseries, including the Nursery Education Grant, Job Centre Plus, Care to Learn, college places and any other streams of funding.	As the leader, I must set the scene regarding how parents should be welcomed, what information to provide and the right attitude.
Sort out parental complaints?	Sometimes. It depends on the nature of the complaint.	I need a complaints procedure in place, in line with Ofsted requirements. Any communication needs to be swift and clear.	Our complaints procedure meets the Ofsted guidance and is clearly displayed for parents to see on the Parents' Board.

Do I . . .?	Is it a regular task?	What skills and knowledge do I need to do this?	What makes this a leadership task?
Complete an induction with new staff member?	I am part of this, but it's not just me.	I need an induction process in place and need to know . how to retain staff and maintain good HR practice.	As the leader, I must ensure there is a process in place.
Sort out staffing issues?	This depends on the stage. For example, I am on the appeals panel for grievance and disciplinary. Much can be done early on, but it depends on when and where the issues arise. Resolving bigger organisational issues, such as pension and pay awards, are my responsibility.	I need to have a good set of HR policies including fair and robust recruitment policies. Legally compliant contracts and terms and conditions are critical and need regular reviews. I have developed competencies for staff members including identifying what they are expected to do.	Issues are best solved by me or the immediate manager. Often all that is needed is time, space and a quiet cup of tea to let someone clear the air. I am always involved in procedures and And responsible for continual ways of improving things for staff.
Complete staff appraisals and training?	No, I delegate this where possible to line management. However, setting the learning and development ethos and practice is part of my job.	I use a Performance Management Policy to help me do this, as it lays out what is expected of staff and they can also see what they are being measured against.	Staff development is part of my role as the leader, in order to keep staff happy and motivated.
Collect money and buy staff birthday presents?	Sometimes, but often I've got a willing volunteer who loves this job. Hallelujah!	I need to understand how these little touches are critical for staff motivation. I have a system for remembering staff birthdays and for remembering those who for religious or personal reasons do not celebrate birthdays. The person in charge of the birthday kitty is brilliant at getting just the right card and present.	As the leader, I am all about motivation, inspiration and finding as many ways as possible of creating an emotionally intelligent environment.

Do I . . .?	Is it a regular task?	What skills and knowledge do I need to do this?	What makes this a leadership task?
Observe staff and students and give feedback?	I complete at least one observation of each staff member before supervision, as a basis for discussion.	I understand how to conduct an observation in line with Ofsted requirement. I use a form that helps to record evidence as basis of feedback. I am able to assess levels of engagement with children.	I try to lead from the front but try and balance this with not getting bogged down in the details. Having a student can be very refreshing and introduces me to new ideas, which keeps me up to date.
Coach students?	Yes, I employ a student social worker every year to do this. I think leaders need to give something back to the sector and having a student is one way of doing this.	I need to understand curriculum requirements and the student's targets and how to ensure I can give the student the best possible experience.	It's part of a leader's responsibility to share knowledge and learn about modern practices.
Attend training?	Yes, I also like to take a member of staff with me to conferences. It is good quality thinking time.	Where possible I attend training courses and conferences in line with new ideas, practices, research and legislation. Conferences are a good place to network and briefing meetings are good for seeking information about imminent changes.	As the leader, I need to be informed and one step ahead so the organisation stays on course and remains up to date, responsive and compliant.
Read research and new guidance papers and submit comments?	Yes, but I could improve my ability to write a paper – though I was delighted when I had a paper published.	I need to move away from the 'domestics' which I can hide behind to avoid coming out of my comfort zone.	I must be informed, because the best settings are those run by leaders who are informed and knowledgeable and turn research into practice.
Read sector publications?	Yes, on the bus.	I like to cut out the useful information and share tips. A good relationship with a magazine is critical for marketing your organisation.	I need information and this is one way of getting it. I need to understand the power of the press in helping them promote

Do I . . .?	Is it a regular task?	What skills and knowledge do I need to do this?	What makes this a leadership task?
			their message and advertise and celebrate their organisations.
Complete e-training?	Yes. I wanted my staff to do it, so felt I had to as well. I found the CAF training online very good.	I had to learn about passwords, logging in, and saving the work so I could come back to it. Since then I have completed a health and safety course online.	As the leader, I need to show new ways of doing things, and the best way to assess their suitability is to try them out.
Go home and write an assignment?	Yes, but I tend to leave it to the last minute.	I need to have a good system for organising myself. I have read up on study skills and can now more effectively speed read and summarise information.	What would the staff say if I failed or did not complete my course?

Case study

Case studies are provided as examples of situations commonly faced by staff. They can be used at a staff team meeting or training session to provoke discussion and get staff to think about how they would respond and what skills, knowledge and understanding they would use and why.

A parent comes to see you complaining that their child is learning nothing and spends all the time playing and tidying up. In addition, the parent says that she never sees her key person and has not had a child development meeting for a long time.

What decision do you take? Explain the process for making the decisions and consider how it will support continual improvement of the setting.

Remember to cover the following:

- What information will you need?
- Where will you get reliable and sufficient evidence for your decisions?
- What barriers may affect you getting information?

3 Leading change

The challenges to successful leadership are many given the complexity of the task. However, I believe that managing change is the greatest challenge, as it requires leaders to apply a range of skills and knowledge in order to reshape systems and services while also bringing people on board who are experiencing a range of emotions, from acceptance to resistance.

Good leadership requires us to recognise these challenges and, where possible, have an option that will help us address the situation so we get the outcome we want as painlessly and positively as possible.

Organisational change

Gandhi said that you have to be the change you want to see; therefore the leader needs to be able to communicate the required change at every level and in as many ways as possible, irrespective of the type of change it is.

There are two main types of organisational change: strategic and operational. Strategic change relates to the future direction of the setting affecting one or more goals. It involves some major switch in what the setting does and how it does it, and usually takes place over a period of years. It can include growth, innovation and diversification. Operational or day-to-day change happens constantly and is often minor and incremental. In essence, change means:

- Learning something new
- Unlearning what you already know and can do
- Challenging your personal attitudes.

When implementing change, leaders and managers are either making or responding to events that require change and adjustments to work practice and the management of the setting. It is a familiar feature of the early years sector. Change is one of the few certainties in early years, and a competent and effective early years leader must understand how to lead change and harness, focus and orchestrate everyone so they are moving positively towards the common purpose – that is, the change you want to see happen.

Most important, though often not considered, is the fact that early years leaders need to create a climate in which children also learn to cope with change.

We are working in difficult times, ever changing and shifting . . . beyond our ability to predict, for the future has become difficult to govern. I believe that the challenge facing children today is to think how to interconnect – this is the watchword for the present and the future – a word that we need to understand deeply and in all its forms.

(Malaguzzi, 2005, p. 1)

Change can be scary but it doesn't have to be and when it comes from the front line it can be very healthy. Many people see change as a negative process because it involves engaging with the unknown; but this is not always the case. Change can be a stimulus for new ideas and can rekindle enthusiasm and commitment. As Richard Hooker said: "Change is not made without inconvenience, even from worse to better." That is surely the case, even now.

All organisations, including early years settings, need to be able to respond to change in order to remain competitive and viable. Those leading an early years organisation will know what it feels like to have to react, reform and renew themselves in order to respond quickly and successfully to frequent political, social and economic upheavals that can affect their funding, support and requirements. All this is very unsettling for staff and requires the leader to keep the organisation running smoothly despite the changes.

Staff have to be able to continually reflect and review their service, to ensure that it is meeting both the needs of those using it and those of potential users – and, by doing this, they are creating a culture that takes change for granted and is a normal occurrence. In fact, most change that occurs within a setting is instigated from within. There are, of course, other times when major strategic changes are imposed because of economic or legislative issues. This could be reacting to new challenges, for example, taking two year olds from the Government funded two-year-old programme, getting all early years leaders to be graduates, implementing the revised Early Years Foundation Stage 2014 (EYFS) curriculum, or adapting to the changing Ofsted inspection regime, to list but a few. So in the spirit that change is the only constant, below is a reminder of recent changes in early years.

Summary of early years change

1998 12.5 free hours of childcare for all four year olds

1999 Sure Start programme launched

2000 Ofsted inspections for the early years introduced under the Care Standards Act (enacted 2002)

2003 Intentions to create a Sure Start Children's Centre in every community announced

2004 Free entitlements to 12.5 hours of early education extended to all three year olds ('ten year strategy for childcare') with commitments including:

- New qualification system
- Reformed regulatory framework and inspection regime
- Introduction of Transformation Fund (later 'Graduate Leaders Fund' to support the development and professionalism of the workforce)

2006 Early Years Foundation Stage (EYFS) curriculum developed under the Childcare Act

2010 Free entitlement extended to 15 hours for all three and four year olds

2011 Dame Clare Tickell's 'The Early Years: Foundations for Life, Health and Learning' published

2012 Professor Cathy Nutbrown's 'Foundation for Quality' published

2013 Government publishes responses to the Nutbrown review: the 'More Great Childcare' and 'More Affordable Childcare' policies include the following intentions:

- Financial help for working parents to meet the costs of childcare
- Strengthening the inspection regime by making Ofsted the sole arbitrator of quality
- Reforming early years qualifications through the introduction of Early Years Educators and Early Years Teachers

2013 Free entitlement to 15 hours for 20% of two year olds who are most disadvantaged

2014 From September, free entitlement extended to 15 hours for the 40% most dis-advantaged two year olds

2014 Children and Families Act introducing the Child-minding Agencies proposal.

Leading the change

The problem with the future is that it is here before we know it. The future tends to catch us unawares and it's upon us before we are really ready for it. The leadership role is key to successful change management and, in order to lead and manage the change cycle effectively, the leader needs be able to adapt to the change positively and understand the process. This means being very informed and sensitive to those people affected by the change (no matter how limited the effect is). Leaders need to understand how change affects staff and how this in turn can impact on the running of the setting. Leaders have to find a way to maintain a sense of purpose so that the staff feel safe and know where they are being lead. Leading change can be an art rather than a science and so responses are not predictable. It is therefore useful to have some sense of the patterns that help make changes successful, while also keeping a balance and responding to the actual situation. Ultimately, leaders need to motivate staff to accept the change and subsequently to actually want it!

No matter whether change is good or bad, people will generally resist it. Interestingly, in 1927, psychologist Elton Mayo discovered that output increased every time a change was made to working conditions. Also, absenteeism declined by 80% during the period of change. The explanation he gave is that people respond to attention. Taking part in experiments and cooperating in changes heightens interest, team spirit and self-esteem, regardless of what the change actually is. Therefore a few changes can make all the difference between a boring work environment and a stimulating one. However, too many changes will leave staff overwhelmed. In a survey by Roffey Park Management Agenda in 2008, two-thirds of the firms believed that managing change was their biggest challenge. They described the common pitfalls of managing change as:

- Failure to maintain momentum (58%)
- Failure to consolidate benefits (64%)
- Failure to manage employee motivation (65%)
- Failure to learn from any changes (71%).

In addition, 37% of employers rated their organisation's leadership negatively, despite acknowledging that development was the most useful means of facilitating successful leadership. And a worrying 55% of employers failed actively to develop leadership at all levels. They recognised that change increased stress for leaders as well as creating internal politics. The inevitable increased workload as a result of driving a change forward was the biggest challenge, and made managers cranky and irritable. This led to low motivation, higher sickness absence, reduced performance, low morale and a breakdown in working relationships.

Poor management of the change will lead to a de-motivated staff team, with all the usual consequences of low morale, including tired staff, absenteeism, an increased number of mistakes, confusion, and greater chances of conflict in the setting.

It is not surprising that people fear change, because it can have any of the following outcomes, all of which could be significant:

- Change can affect knowledge and skill requirements
- Change can cause financial or status loss
- Change can elicit a jealous response from others who may feel that it could result in their loss of esteem
- Change can involve risk and increase the possibility of failure
- Change can involve alterations to social relationships.

As Charles Darwin said, 'It is not the change which we resist, it is the threat which fills us with fear.' It is part of a leader's role to try to reduce any feelings of threat. A successful leader will also recognise that every staff member will have a personal response to the change and their response cannot be predicted. Most people will have experienced different levels of change in their workplace, and if their experiences have been poor this will have an impact on how they respond to new change. For example, if staff have not made a fuss, it is necessary not to make the mistake of thinking they have accepted the change: quiet defiance is a much harder problem to deal with. The most important message to remember is that organisations are full of 'change survivors' – people who have learned to live through organisational change without actually developing themselves.

Common responses to change

Below is a list of common responses to change. Some people may not experience any of these responses, others a few and a small number of people may go through each and every phase.

- Shock (Will I have a job?)
- Anxiety (How will I cope with this? It is all too much)
- Denial (I will just ignore it and if I say no often enough they will go away)
- Resistance (It will never work)
- Fear of overload (I can't manage my work now, how will I do this as well?)
- Low morale (This is all too much, they do not care about the staff)
- Awareness (OK, I recognise it is needed but how will I manage it?)
- Incompetence and fear of failure (I can't do this)
- Sense of loss of control (I will look stupid if I can't do this and I am supposed to be senior)
- Acceptance (I will try, maybe it is possible)
- Testing/searching for meaning (I will start to read the plan and understand what I have to do)
- Understanding and adjustments (Let's get on with it, it's not so bad)
- Integration (It is OK now; I can work within this).

Sharon Turnbull (2008) referred to the concept of diagnostic change using two key dimensions: the committed and the critical. She described them as follows:

Committed = commitment of an individual to the success of the organisation.
Critical = individual's willingness to ask searching questions.

She used these dimensions to identify how some staff will respond to change, which is useful when plotting a change strategy. I think you will recognise some if not all of the people below.

'The evangelists' are intensely loyal, take corporate change at face value, are highly committed and deeply uncritical. They are always keen to adopt and implement new initiatives. As a result their expectations of their leader are very high and they would not dream of questioning their leader's judgement or ask probing questions. This is all good except, their capitulation can give you a very false reading of the situation and can fool you into thinking change has bedded in successfully. You are therefore less prepared when reality hits and you discover that the change has not embedded itself quite as successfully as they led you to believe.

'The actors' are equally uncritical, but much less committed than the evangelists, and this might confuse you at first glance. Both lead you to think they have accepted the changes and the new message, but actors are chameleons: they would never dissent in case it gets them into trouble, but they have deeply sceptical views with no true loyalty and will change allegiances quite quickly.

Finally, there are the 'untouched professionals', whose loyalty lies with their profession rather than the organisation. They feel untouched by programmes that sell values, visions and missions, since their own values are embedded in their professional identities. Committed to their roles rather than to their employer, they are unlikely to engage with the programme themselves, remaining ambivalent and showing only a polite passing interest in the changes. The problem the leader has with them is the negative impact of their ambivalence on those around them.

Understanding why people resist change is important in terms of developing a strategy for reducing resistance or dealing with it. Remember some people will be overwhelmed by their self-interests, while others will not be able to operate in the new world because they are fearful. And there are always some people who will just hate the change and disagree with it no matter what. It is important to remember that this group of people can make others frightened or resistant by instigating rumour and innuendo, especially when the staff are fearful of job cuts. In bigger organisations the situation is exacerbated when angry and disaffected staff start playing politics.

Kotter (1999) gave a few ideas as to how to manage the resistance. These included: communicating, educating, involving, facilitating, negotiating, manipulating and using explicit and implicit coercion. He also pointed out that these approaches could sometimes take a long time or fail. This is reassuring because it feels more realistic when tackling the issue. If someone cannot take on what you want, then sometimes the only way is out.

It is important not to confuse resistance to change with straightforward conflict and aggression. When I asked my own group of managers what they liked least about leading and managing, they all said that dealing with conflict was their least favourite task. I would agree that managing conflict is stressful and uncomfortable. However, despite the fact that we all dislike managing it, we seem very capable of creating it. No doubt we have all encountered its manifestations in terms of moody staff, grumpy unpleasantness, disregard and downright rudeness, quiet aggression, sullenness, carping and gossiping, isolating colleagues, and failure to do as required as soon as your back is turned. The list is endless and material for many a soap opera, which is why we are never truly prepared for the results of conflict and why there are so few rules to manage it. The first challenge for a leader is to spot it, as often conflict smoulders and unless you are around and tuned in you can miss it. A common response is to wait until it blows over. I have tried that technique often and, while it works in some situations, more often than not it does not and the consequences seem more dramatic than if I had addressed it straightaway. Hindsight is a great thing. (See Chapter 4 for ways to deal with conflict in early years settings.)

There are two ways of responding which leaders need to consider in order to successfully manage change. Firstly, you need to be able to manage the actual change project on a short-term basis and on a more long-term basis you need to create an organisation that is ready for change and not fazed by it. This is particularly important in the world of early years, as things change when a new child enters the class as much as when a government announces a new strategy or approach to teaching. For example, in early years many staff become leaders because they are excellent practitioners with children. As they move up the ladder they find themselves working with children less and less and doing a different job involving admin, data collection and finance. One of the most unpopular tasks is managing finance. This is not just operational finance in the shape of budgets, fee collection and payroll, but actually bidding for funds to keep the setting afloat. At one stage, leaders of voluntary and private-sector settings had to bid for funds from 55 different streams, each with a different set of funding criteria and monitoring requirements. However, failure to access the funds could be the difference between sustainability for the year and financial ruin and closure. Managing finance is a steep learning curve for many, and successful leaders are those able to rise to this challenge, identify and access funds and use the funding to improve the quality of the service in a way that secured the setting and provided stability for the staff and children.

Secondly, given that settings are constantly subject to change, you need to to create a dynamic learning environment and an organisational culture that allows staff to embrace change and does not immediately reject the possibility of any change. These settings tend to be goal-directed and purposeful and change becomes a habit for everyone. They have a clear balance between autonomy and control and the constraints are defined and accepted. Staff know what they can do and what is expected of them. Leaders inspire the team and foster creativity and innovation in the setting. The development of the setting is a continual activity and change is part of the improvement process. This has a positive knock-on effect as settings with a high emphasis on supporting and developing staff seem to be places where staff stay and remain motivated. This is critical because another problem facing leaders in early years is how to retain staff and keep them happy and motivated. Other sectors have similar challenges as noted in a study conducted by Roffey Park (2008) of 479 managers, which found that employers saw retention, recruitment and skills shortages as massive challenges for the future. In response, managers thought leadership ability was the most useful tool. Of the respondents, 65% cited their ability to develop senior leaders as crucial, while 30% said talent management and knowledge management would be key.

In early years, governments talk expansively about how they want to create a world-class children's workforce. Policies are developed to create a workforce to which people aspire and thrive, where they can develop their skills and build satisfying and rewarding careers, and in which parents, carers, children and young people can place trust and respect. It's a perfectly correct aspiration and one to which leaders should aspire. The journey to achieve it is somewhat more difficult because the current workforce is ill-prepared for it and the ambitions and the reality of being able to afford to develop such a workforce is challenging. Instead, while the Government espouses a great deal of rhetoric about the importance of a highly trained workforce, the reality is that it is left down to employers to create the opportunities.

Think and reflect!

Do you think you lead change successfully?

The questionnaire below has been completed by a hypothetical leader. Have a go at answering the questions yourself and use the answers to assess your own leadership. Perhaps you could make an action plan to improve the areas which are weaker or missing!

Do you . . .?	Can you give an example?	Really?
Create an environment with a culture of ongoing learning and ensure this is written as part of the principles of the setting?	I have introduced the principle that learning and research is critical to the continuing quality of the service. I have developed a set of research cluster groups to examine better ways of doing things in the nursery. I have allocated funds in the budget to ensure I can pay for staff to have at least two days on a Continuing Professional Development (CPD) programme.	I organised an annual staff questionnaire and asked staff what keeps them with us. A majority answered that it was the training and development opportunities and their ability to be able to try new things.
Create a climate in which it is safe for individuals to try out different ways of doing things, to contribute more fully and to have a greater share in what is going on in the setting?	I have introduced regular working groups and sounding boards in the evening with pizza and wine. The idea is for a group of staff to discuss what they think is working well and what needs tweaking.	The sounding board meetings for staff to share ideas and comments which are run after work get an 80% attendance every time and useful feedback.
Communicate openly and frankly, encouraging ideas and testing them out so staff know what happens to their ideas?	The monthly newsletter includes examples of good practice, well done to teams and lots of photos. We have also submitted articles to sector magazines.	Yes but I could use the website more for this also.
Make decisions nearer to the information point rather than referring up through the hierarchy?	Decision-making is delegated to managers who are expected to make decisions within the organisation's policies and procedures which they have had the chance to contribute to and amend. When they are uncertain or facing new non-urgent situations they bring the conundrum to the support group for discussion and debate.	I recently introduced critical reviews to examine new situations and decision-making processes and this has been helpful in identifying how we ensure consistent application across the organisation. I need managers to get braver at delegating decision-making to staff and then stopping themselves from overriding the decisions. It's causing a bit of tension.

Do you . . .?	Can you give an example?	Really?
Value people's contribution, stressing interdependence?	*I know this is very important, but sometimes it is hard to value some of the ill-thought-out ideas that are put forward. I have tried to encourage the idea of tests and pilots so that weak ideas fail early and then after a review can be changed or stopped without dampening enthusiasm.*	*New ideas that came from staff included an improved outings form and putting the activities plan template on the back of observation sheets. These ideas have been adopted. Staff who show an interest are invited to external conferences and 'social dos' as a way of thanking them for wanting to improve the service.*
Encourage staff to be curious, well informed, up to date and interested to know what is going on in the world outside their settings?	*I have begun to invite staff members to attend relevant external events with me and that has been surprisingly well received. I must get better at preparing them so we can all make the best of the opportunity.*	*I get regular texts from staff about something they have read or seen on TV which may be of interest. We also have a long queue of staff interested in doing a degree.*
Put systems in place to regularly publicise and celebrate the achievements of colleagues as they respond to and deal with change?	*I use all the usual channels but need to think more about ways of communicating. I use what I can, including emails, memos and newsletters. I think I might try a change update to show everyone what has happened so far.*	*There can never be enough praise, especially as the organisation grows and new changes are bedded in.*

Strategic change preparation plan

Use the change preparation plan below to help get ready to lead a major strategic change. Do this with your senior team. Consider the good practice suggestions and think how they would work for you. Agree the actions needed to implement the strategic change, identify the resistance and how you will manage this. Think of some quick wins, things that are easy to do and give an instant impact. This really helps to mitigate some resistance as people see you are serious about listening to them and doing some of the things they have requested. Check outcomes. Are they the ones you want? Some outcomes are a surprise and can be both positive and negative.

The completed plan below uses the example of a leader implementing the revised Special Education Needs and Disability Code of Practice 2014.

Good practice suggestions	Action steps	Challenges and possible impact	Quick wins	Outcome
Make only the necessary changes. Keep some things stable.	Find allies who will support the change and help you implement it. Get someone who has been through a similar change elsewhere to talk to the staff.	Information overload. Incorrect understanding, panic and paralysis.	Update SEN operations file Show staff that it is not quite so different from what they do now.	Updated policies and procedures. Ready for Ofsted.
Reassure staff about the impact of the change. Be open and honest and tell them how it will affect their jobs.	Set up a series of information change workshops for SENCOs and then a plan to cascade it across the organisation.	Objection, rejection, anger, fear and sabotage.	Give those who are complaining the loudest a key role in the change management.	First stage of change plan introduced.
Give credit to people's fears and concerns.	Do this throughout. Do not dismiss staff's fears even if they sound ridiculous. Counter claims and anxieties with fact and balance. Be calm and kind.	The doubters and objectors will want to see the project fail so keep tabs on them. If necessary use a stick-and-carrot approach.	Give personal replies, so there is little chance of information being corrupted. Have a celebration package for every step staff take. Give little treats along the way.	More chance of success.
Provide clear, accurate, useful information, both orally and in writing, and use every medium available.	Use guidance information issued through the Foundation Stage website.	Ensure everyone understands the information by using relevant language and images.	Staff workshop. The best way to learn is to teach.	Better informed staff and parents. Nice evidence for Ofsted.
If you are giving others the responsibility to share information make sure they know exactly what to say and can cope with the questions. If in doubt, do all the briefings yourself.	Practise presenting the information and answering questions by using role-play. Make a PowerPoint presentation for staff to use.	Inability to answer questions or just getting the wrong end of the stick.	Thank you cards to staff. Invite one of them to present outside the setting, if they feel able to. Good learning and development opportunities.	Good piece of professional development. Details included in staff personal records of achievement.

Good practice suggestions	Action steps	Challenges and possible impact	Quick wins	Outcome
Plan how to keep the information flowing – small chunks and often.	Provide a standard display. Use photos that show the changes, as people are visual.	Information everywhere, yet no one reads it.	Produce a Special Educational and Disability handbook to keep all information together and accessible.	Moving towards plan to implement the revised SEND step by step.
Involve the staff. Really listen to people, rather than just saying that people can share their views.	Have a lunch with staff to get their feedback. Have a reply section to questions on the display. Have an email slot for staff to write their views in.	Feedback from whingers can have negative impact, so this needs to be managed.	Quality time with staff. Useful information.	Positive relationship building.
eBe visible and walk the job so people can talk to you.	Visit a setting, area or room at least once a week. Don't just fly in and out. Stay and chat.	Time, time, time!	Immediate reactions good and bad.	More relevant information as you judge for yourself.
If the change pertains to a special group, e.g. Sencos, work with them directly.	Have them present their progress to relevant group, e.g. trustees.	Giving them time out of the nursery to get them together can be difficult.	Quality time to develop a new idea.	Better cascading of information.
Tell the story of the change in as many ways as possible. Show staff videos of what you want the change to look like. Make it real so it is not so scary, especially if it involves IT!	Update the website (if you have one) with progress. Many parents use this and it will be a helpful message to those who may be concerned about their children.	Lack of IT skills and equipment. Little funding for marketing and communication. Multi-sites and difficulty cascading information.	Piece of evidence to show any inspection authority on the progress you have made.	Better use and control of IT.
Have a programme of support, coaching and training in place. Have a range because everyone has a different learning style and a range of sources of information will help this.	Draw in favours from everyone, to give you the capacity to give as much one-to-one support as possible. Seek the advice of your local authority.	The coaches do not support the plans and the staff get mixed messages.	The coaches support you at no cost, so the change is accepted and implemented with a positive attitude.	More advocates for the service.

Good practice suggestions	Action steps	Challenges and possible impact	Quick wins	Outcome
Have a pilot and try the change out in a small controlled group first.	Test the new forms.	Transition from existing records. Ability of staff to explain change to parents.	Invite the Area Senco to a SENCO meeting and ask the Senco to present the work done to ensure the new SEND is in place. Celebrate!	Compliant setting.
Plan a celebration.	Launch the change. Have a day when it all kicks in. Give it a focus.	Negative vibes, little staff engagement. Looks like it is 'your' change rather than 'our' change.	Good PR for the setting. Boost staff morale.	Job done.

Think and reflect!
Change strategy checklist

Use the list below as a checklist or the basis of your strategy for change.

- Prepare the staff
- Let them know how the plan will look after the change
- Be honest and flexible
- Involve the staff in the process
- Have frequent formal and informal meetings
- Tune in to the ideas, views and feelings of others
- Manage rumour and conflict
- Ask insightful questions
- Communicate little and often and in as many ways as possible
- Listen attentively and respect feelings
- Be enthusiastic and positive
- Be pragmatic, rarely will something go completely to plan
- Find out who supported the change and who resisted it, and talk to those who were against it

- Look after those leading the change
- Celebrate the new and do not dismissthe past
- Find someone to support you – it can be lonely at the top.

Managing change checklist

Having introduced the change, you now need to check it has been implemented. Use this checklist to assess progress.

Question	Yes – how do I know?	No – how do I know?	Change indicators
Have I checked that everyone knows why we are making the change? Am I sure?	I gave a quiz and they were all able to answer. Key questions on the door before they left the staff meeting.		Staff using the new language of change.
Do the staff know the benefits of the change? How do I know for sure?	I think so, they could see how it would improve children's records and liked the emphasis on care and education together.	I am not sure about the two deputies – a little confused.	Putting the information into a presentation for parents. Using some of the concepts very well.
Do the staff know how it will affect them? Am I sure?	Yes, this was their concern about having to use new documentation for observations and planning.		New planning tools to be used.
Can everyone answer the question, 'What is in it for me?'	I think so. They all seem to think it will reduce separate workloads if they communicate well enough.	Sally M seems a little stuck. Will need to arrange a one-to-one meeting for her.	Better balance of work. Simpler planning and updated welfare policies.
Is the action plan working?	Yes. We have all used it.		Lots of ticks.
Is there enough communication? Have I missed anyone? Am I sure?	I am never sure there is enough of a mixture. I still hear questions that we have answered again and again.	I need a system to involve two staff who were on long-term absence.	Used as many ways of communication as I could think of. Kept remembering different learning styles and visual images were important.

Question	Yes – how do I know?	No – how do I know?	Change indicators
Am I coping with the change myself? Do I need help?	I am tired of trying to ensure we are on target. It would be useful to have someone come in and do an objective assessment.		New planning documentation, updated policies and the learning journey are all operational.
Am I checking progress weekly? Am I sure I am asking the right questions and getting useful feedback?	The staff are asking for new resources which are relevant.	I need to do more. I cannot allow this to slip. I must keep on this.	Feedback is positive and shows progress. We are talking about tweaking new approaches.
What else do I need to consider?	I must check parents are getting the relevant information. Check Self Evaluation Forms (SEFs).		SEFs included the implementation of the EYFS as an objective.

Activity to complete at a staff team meeting or training session

This activity can be used at a staff meeting or training session to provoke discussion and get staff to think about how they would respond and what skills, knowledge and understanding they would use and why.

You want to introduce the concept of cohort tracking into the nursery. You know that staff will give this a mixed reaction and it will raise a number of questions. Using the plan, identify the challenges and the strategy you will use to apply them in order to best manage the change.

Change target : To develop a new way of tracking children's entry level ability for language and social skills once they start nursery

Action needed	Who will do this and by when?	What resources will be needed? (training/finance/time)	Communication methods to staff, children and parents (as many ways as possible and as often as possible)	Possible problem (delays/snags)	Possible solution	Success indicator (how will we know when the change has happened?)
Identify key measure we will track and develop a form to capture the information	Jane the EY lead. First draft by 23rd of the month in time for next planning Meeting.	Two hours non-contact time. Feedback from each key person.	Plans to be simple and clear and aligned to children's learning journey assessment format.	Shortage of non-contact time due to staff holidays. Lack of information about all the children's interests and stage of readiness for the activities. Limited resources.	Combining two units together for an hour to release at least one staff member to support Jane. Manager to talk to local authority advisor for examples of key indicators. New copy of Mary Sheridan's developmental milestone book, *From Birth to Five Years*.	Completed activity forms, readily accessible and which parents and staff understand.

4 Overcoming leadership challenges

In this chapter I want to focus on the three particular issues research tells us are the most challenging for leaders in all the sectors, not just early years. These are:

- Communication – the ability to communicate a message effectively
- Decision-making – the ability to make decisions
- Conflict – dealing with conflict.

That said, there are myriad challenges to leaders and some come all at once, but this chapter looks at the three listed above. I have collected together what I consider to be helpful guidance, ideas and suggestions offered by a range of people to enable leaders to consider how best to respond.

Of course in highlighting these three issues I am not suggesting that other concerns are not equally important and taxing. Issues such as staff management and motivation and keeping up to speed with new ideas and developments are a continual challenge and considered in later chapters. Managing change merited a whole chapter given the significance of the leader in the change process and a successful outcome.

Communication

Communication seems such an obvious thing, but for leaders it has disproportionate significance when they do not get it right. Siraj-Blatchford and Mani (2007) found that early years leaders who encouraged and created effective communication among the staff were more successful at imparting their vision which led to the vision being better understood and consequently embedded more consistently by staff in all areas of practice in the setting. In late 2008, MPs were asked what was critical for a successful prime minister. The answer: the ability to communicate, persuade and enthuse, otherwise the message was lost. Wise words! Leaders are judged on their ability to communicate at every level as an individual as well as the head of a service, team or organisation. There is an expectation that leaders need to be great orators as well as good listeners, able to write and communicate through presentations and also tell the story. It is quite a daunting task and many leaders need a bit of help to get it right.

In 1992, when researcher Warren Bennis introduced the concept of leadership competency, he pressed for four competences, quoted by Tomlinson (2004) as:

1 Management of attention: the communication of an extraordinary focus of commitment which attracts people to leaders.

2 Management of meaning: the communication of a leader's vision, making their dreams apparent to others and aligning people with them.

3 Management of trust: the main determinant of which is reliability and constancy.

4 Management of self: knowing one's skills and deploying them effectively – without which leaders can do more harm than good.

(Tomlinson, 2004, p. 127)

Clearly, Bennis saw communication as critical. He maintained leaders were the focus of attention and how they presented themselves to people was significant in terms of how people responded. As leaders, therefore, we have to accept that our personal presentation is critical.

> ## Think and reflect!
>
> When we communicate, words convey 7% of the message, tone conveys 38% and body language, 55%. Words are the least important factor in oral communication. Do you think before you speak?

The art of communication

In order to communicate well you need to consider the audience, the information you want to share, the context within which you are communicating and how you will present the message. It never ceases to amaze me how what seems like a clear message is completely misread even though there are only two people in the conversation. The chance of this happening at a meeting hugely increases. I used to send a list of action points to the nursery managers who had sent a representative to meetings as we always had a bet as to how wrong some people got the message. Therefore, in order to guarantee the best chance of getting it right, consider doing the following:

- Prepare
- Think through what you want to say
- Be authentic, people prefer to hear the truth
- Remember who you are talking to
- Try to be clear and concise, and avoid jargon

- Sound as if you know what you are talking about
- Be honest – don't make up the answer; say you are not sure and you will find out
- Listen
- Show your interest by looking and sounding interested
- Confirm you both understand what you discussed, especially if the conversation included a request.

Nowadays, communication is even more of a challenge with the use of technology. There is what I think of as 'death by email' and the expectation that, because an email is sent in a nanosecond, you should get or give an equally immediate response. Email is dangerous because when you click on Send you enter the point of no return. The number of people who send emails without thinking through the message, either lacing it with sarcasm or just an angry rant still amazes me. I suggest you open your emails no more than twice a day. Don't jump to respond every time you hear a ping and think long and hard before you press Send. Consider the attachments and who needs to be copied in. Does everyone need to be involved in the correspondence? Is there any real reason for copying certain people in? Finally, and this is just my idiosyncrasy, I treat emails as a form of letter so I always begin them with a greeting and end them with a salutation. I have no time for people sending emails as if they were part of their stream of consciousness. It strikes me as bad manners. And sending an email in anger, well, you are just looking for trouble!

When writing your communication policy, remember to consider all the modern ways staff use technology including Facebook, LinkedIn, Twitter, Flikr and YouTube. There are many risks regarding how information can be shared using these methods and reputation risk is high.

Meetings

Leaders rely on their credibility to win the respect of colleagues and meetings are one of those places where leaders are on show. Meetings are never the place to look or sound ill-prepared, be unable to answer questions or interpret the information shared. Not only is there a risk to professional credibility but there is a chance that the failure to interpret the information at the meeting may be detrimental; for example, losing out on critical funding or the opportunity to sign up for a key policy-making opportunity with long-term benefits for the organisation. Sometimes it is hard to stay focused until the end of a meeting as some of the information seems inappropriate or not useful, especially if it is a difficult meeting where people are complaining, moaning and keen to disrupt and distract at every opportunity. The stalwart leader will stick with it because often it is what is not said that is the issue rather than what is! What, for example, would happen if you, the leader, failed to notice an agreement to reduce the nursery grant funding or open a free school right next to your half-full play group?

Everyone in a leadership position has to run meetings. Sometimes, this feels like all we ever do. Therefore we must learn to run effective meetings that extend our credibility and get things done. Some simple pointers for chairing a successful and productive meeting include:

- Be prepared and read the agenda and the minutes so you are familiar with who will attend and the outstanding action points. Don't leave yourself to the mercy of the unknown.

- Ensure information about existing arrangements and structures, and new ideas and opportunities is presented in a variety of ways so as to take account of the different ways people learn and assimilate information.

- Listen to what people are saying both through their words and body language and follow their cues.

- Make yourself heard and command authority to keep order without shouting or getting irritated (not always easy!).

- Ask questions and interpret the answers so it is clear that those attending the meeting actually understand. (Some meetings, in particular those run by local authority colleagues, rely on jargon and acronyms to the bafflement of many a visitor.)

- Manage the meeting so that you avoid information overload (hence controlling the agenda from the outset).

- Encourage participation but manage domination. Try and give everyone a go.

- Summarise the decisions and ensure the minute-taker has captured the main points.

- Conclude clearly and try to finish on time.

If you are at a meeting either seeking information to make a decision or to impart news of a decision, be ready and prepared. Rehearse the pros and cons in advance and think laterally. If you know the members of the group attending, try and anticipate what they may know or feel about the issue and how that may influence the decision you want. At the same time, don't close your mind and think that your way is the best way. Some of my best decisions were made at meetings where people presented some interesting and thought-provoking information which resulted in my doing something completely different with great success.

If you are sending someone to represent you at a meeting, choose carefully. Ensure they have the knowledge and experience to contribute and the ability and motivation to behave in a way that will get a positive outcome. Give them the authority to make decisions, but also give them a let-out clause if they find the process more complex. This is particularly important when it is a high-level meeting where a decision is needed regarding policy, funding or something that will have a significant impact on your setting.

Getting new ideas

Some people say there is no point in having a meeting unless it is to get new ideas. They argue that having meetings to give information is counterproductive and we should be looking at other more interesting and effective ways to do this.

As a leader you can decide when, how and what type of meetings you want to have. You may not be popular with your choice and may get little buy-in from those staff attending the meeting. However, you could sell the idea of meetings in a slightly more creative way and introduce sounding boards, focus groups or brainstorming meetings specifically to generate new ideas or to check out people's views about existing arrangements and structures, and new ideas and opportunities. For example, having sounding boards towards the end of the day with wine and pizza could bring a new perspective on how you want staff to help introduce the new curriculum, or write and develop a parent strategy. Generating a relaxed environment in which individuals feel comfortable and unthreatened helps to draw out new ideas. Try to encourage lateral thinking as well as logical thought to break down and challenge any long-held preconceptions.

These groups are best kept small, with five to nine members who can add ideas to a decision being made. The ideas need to be recorded and shared. Put together all the ideas generated into themes so that you end up with a logical collection of useful information.

Ideas need to be valued and welcomed from all staff, not just senior staff or those whom you value. The more ideas generated the better and good leaders will remember to tell people what they have done with the ideas. Use a whiteboard, newsletter, staff update, website or whatever means you have to thank people for their time and contributions and be very clear how you will use the information. At London Early Years Foundation we use the 'We asked, You said, This Happened' Technique. It's quite a simple approach but it reminds people of the journey.

It can be agreed, therefore, that effective communication is multi-functional, reciprocal and can open up new paths. It involves talking, listening, praising, supporting, clarifying, translating, debating, discussing, and interpreting and understanding the subtle medium of body language. Early years leaders must be able to communicate their vision about how, together, they and their teams can make a difference to children's lives and those of their families.

Making decisions

It is a management truism that the road to hell is paved with good intentions and the road to management and organisational ruin is paved with decisions which have not been implemented or, worse still, have been implemented half-heartedly. It is a wise leader who knows that what they have decided may not be done automatically.

How many times have you heard staff criticise their leaders because they could or would not take a decision so the staff often felt unsafe, unclear and without guidance. It is quite interesting that staff will be more supportive of a leader who makes wrong decisions than one who shirks their responsibility for making decisions and carrying them through.

A decision is a judgement or choice between two or more alternatives and arises in an infinite number of situations from the resolution of a problem to the implementation of a course of action. Managers of people, by definition, must be decision-makers.

(Heller, 1999 p. 154)

We make decisions all day long and some are complex, others routine, some urgent and some can wait. Recently, I have spent a lot of time considering the principle of making a decision by not making one. Aggressive people try and force your hand; some staff are more demanding than others and are not satisfied until something is done, and there are always contract officers ringing up and demanding immediate action. Sometimes the best way to respond is to ask for some time to consider the matter and watch and wait. Think about the 'amygdala hijack', a term coined by Daniel Goleman in his 1996 book *Emotional Intelligence: Why It Can Matter More Than IQ*. He used the term to describe emotional responses from people that are immediate, overwhelming, and out of measure with the actual situation because they have triggered a much more significant emotional threat. These responses often mean that we react or respond in a way that is highly emotional and this does not leave us in control or command of either our emotions or the situation. Goleman recommended a number of personal strategies to avoid this, from a deep breath to a short walk around the room, until we have taken control of the emotional churn and can respond calmly and more rationally. It certainly helps before making a decision.

This matrix of decision-making is a useful tool to review your current process and review whether the way decisions are made in your organisation lead to effective outcomes and actually make a difference to what you do.

<table>
<tr><td></td><td colspan="2" align="center">High urgency</td><td></td></tr>
<tr><td rowspan="2">Low importance</td><td align="center">Decisions that are urgent but not important</td><td align="center">Decisions that are importannt and urgent</td><td rowspan="2">High importance</td></tr>
<tr><td align="center">Decisions that are neither urgent nor important</td><td align="center">Decisions that are important but not urgent</td></tr>
<tr><td></td><td colspan="2" align="center">Low urgency</td><td></td></tr>
</table>

Figure 4.1 Urgency and importance of decisions (Elsevier, Pergamon Flexible Learning, *Decision Making*, 2005)

Top tips

When handling urgent decisions you should:

- Consider the problem
- Get help if possible
- Consider the consequences
- Prioritise and delegate
- Avoid getting sidetracked
- Check progress
- Review the outcome.

Making a decision seems so easy when it is written down in logical steps. Begin with agreeing with yourself and/or others why you need the decision. Check if you have enough information to be balanced and reasoned in your thinking. If you are making a knee-jerk response to something, then be sure the outcome will be worth it. Ask yourself, 'Will the decision meet my objective both now and in the future?', 'Will it solve the problem or help implement the changes I want?', 'What will be the possible outcomes?' Consider the worst-case scenario. If it all went wrong, could you cope? Would the outcome of your decision be worse than the problem you were trying to solve? This is when I imagine a *Sun* headline or facing a board of trustees.

Having made a decision, it needs to be implemented. Can you trust those to whom you will delegate? Do they really understand what you are asking of them? Have you broken the decision into logical steps so they can explain it? Do they understand the actions needed to achieve each step and the deadlines for completing each step? Do they really agree or are they playing along? Remember all the times you have made a decision and found that it has been ignored. So how will you monitor and understand the effects and, when necessary, repeat the process? Making the decision is actually the easy bit but finding a way of checking it is happening and measuring the impact is the bit that often gets lost in the busy day. Having a system to build this in is critical. Failing to act on a decision is often perceived as poor leadership and, in a weak team, staff will take advantage.

> *The most important step in unclogging decision-making bottlenecks is assigning clear roles and responsibilities. Good decision-makers recognise which decisions matter to performance. They think through who should recommend a particular path, who needs to agree, who should have input, who has ultimate responsibility for making the decision and who is accountable for the follow-through. They make the process routine. The result is better coordination and response times.*
> (Rogers, P. and Blenko, M., *Harvard Business Publishing*, 2006)

There are different styles of decision-making and a leader needs to know when to use which style. This is an example given by Heller (2000):

- Autocratic: a decision is taken without consultation, then others are informed of what is to be done and what is expected of them.

- Persuasive: the decision is taken before consultation and then 'sold' to the others.

- Consultative: the views of others are sought and taken into account before the decision is taken.

- Consensus: decisions are taken on a majority basis.

(Heller, 2000, p. 154)

Can you remember a time when you regretted losing your temper and making a hasty autocratic decision because you were fed up with a situation; for example, where staff could not agree on what seemed like a simple issue, such as getting views on managing the Christmas break? I certainly regret times when I insisted on a decision being made, when, with hindsight, I should have kept calm for longer and let the staff sort it out more democratically.

Leaders, especially in busy and demanding settings, may cut short the decision-making process while believing they have given it their full attention. For example, it is easy to hear the first bit of information and not pay enough attention to the whole, because you want the first bit to be the main factor as it fits your own perception and hoped-for outcome. Sometimes, sticking to what you know is the decision rather than looking at what might be improved through an alternative approach. Then, there is the pride-goes-before-a-fall approach, where you do not want to give anyone the satisfaction of saying 'I told you so' and so continue with a bad idea.

Alternatively, a leader who drives most people mad is the one who fails to make a decision and hopes the situation will sort itself out. This is often seen in leaders facing a conflict-driven situation, either with staff or customers and clients. The outcome is rarely positive as the situation drifts, and some leaders delegate the mess to a junior member of staff and then really lose credibility from all concerned for failing to address the issue. An example of this was when a nursery leader failed to talk to a parent about growing debt. Head office intervened and sent out letters threatening to terminate the child's place. The parent became upset and challenged the leader about not talking to them directly and ascertaining the reason. The leader sidestepped the situation by delegating it to the deputy as part of her training. A failure on all fronts and remarkably commonplace.

Think and reflect!
The C-step approach

I like Sergent's C-step approach and have adapted it as an example. It's a simple maxim and sums up the key steps. Use this framework as a basis for decision-making in your setting.

Consider – What is the decision? At a recent meeting a decision had to be made about how we deal with serious incidents in the absence of the leader.

Consult – Who should I speak to? I decided the matter needed to be discussed with all senior staff and some frontline staff, particularly with regards to the communication elements.

Crunch – Having sought the information, how could I best analyse it? I decided on a written one-page procedure, filed in the front of the operations file.

Communicate – Who do I need to inform? All staff needed to understand their role and this was written in the procedure and in a summary in the monthly update and via email.

Check – How effective was my decision? We agreed to review this after the first time it was used and to have an annual review in case new legislation or findings from elsewhere influenced our procedure.

(Adapted from Sergent, 1976)

Things that can go wrong

Decisions frequently go awry, not least because of people's attitude to the change. The statements below capture some of the attitudes that can cause the decision- making process to fail.

- What problem? (Failure to define the problem may be due to: inadequate or insufficient information, lack of analysis, lack of time, people hating the truth or too much information.)
- Would you believe it? What was she/he thinking? Never gets it right . . . Hopeless, never thinks it through . . . So arrogant!
- Will I, won't I? If I do and it's wrong, they will blame me. Oh, I can't bear that . . . Procrastination is best.
- Got two years left; hey ho, not doing anything new . . . just sticking it out.
- Let's just do what we know; we have always done it this way. No we don't need to use technology, just send them a memo.
- Let's just tinker around the edge.
- No, it will be fine; get on and do it and don't think too hard about the consequences.
- Can't take the risk; there's too much at stake.
- Same old, same old . . . what's to decide?
- Who cares? Am I bothered?
- Well I was told it's the decision . . . so get on with it!

As a leader, you may find yourself coming to a decision that is also most likely to expose you to significant risk that could result in you losing your job and reputation; for example, making a decision which takes on employment law or health and safety guidelines which are open to interpretation. Such decisions may include reorganising your team, moving a member of staff, sacking a member of staff, building a huge wooden playground, or embarking on an expensive marketing campaign. In effect, decisions that are complex and high risk. When making such a decision, ask yourself whether you are really committed to it and prepared to take full responsibility for your actions and are ready to face the consequences if you are proven to be wrong, either immediately or in the long term.

Interestingly, leaders who are willing to accept a failure and take it on the chin get more respect than ridicule; people can be very generous in the face of failure. However, if you make a habit of failing, then it will not take long for questions to be asked. Having said that, I know a number of people who have seemed to emerge blemish-free from a series of catastrophes: they were, for the most part, well liked and had gained people's good opinion, which counted in their favour.

In essence the purpose of a decision is to make the best possible choice based on sound information. Problem-solving precedes decision-making, because the decision must be based on the best understanding of the past and present situation. Decisions are valueless until they are translated into positive action.

Dealing with conflict

Managing conflict is probably the least favourite task for all leaders. It is stressful and unpleasant but best dealt with quickly and efficiently as it rarely resolves itself.

The image conjured up by the phrase 'managing conflict' is often that of an aggressive, angry, rude adult demanding and complaining about some aspect of the service. This can be true and leaders do have to deal with some very unpleasant adults at times. However, most work-based conflict is related to staff. According to the Centre for Effective Dispute Resolution (CEDR), one third of managers would rather parachute jump for the first time than resolve a difficult issue. For 69%, the most unpleasant task was addressing an underperforming staff member. This included dealing with people with a negative attitude, such as the continually moaning or sulking staff member, the staff member who doesn't do their work and causes an negative atmosphere which affects other staff, and the staff member who has difficulty accepting their role and responsibility and complains constantly. In today's world where we are asked to improve multi-agency approaches to our work with staff from different professional backgrounds, the risk of conflict is high. The answer appears to lie in finding a coherent philosophy or purpose and getting people to agree to it so the principles really influence practice. Once people buy in, it is harder for them to say 'Well this is not on my agenda' or 'Our developmental plan isn't aligned to this'. Of course, the task of reaching an agreed philosophy is difficult. Many people just want to get on with their job, which is understandable; but then they have less to fall back on when they face an obstacle or conflict. Early years leaders have often resisted going into leadership roles because they are reluctant to take on managing adults, a fact also found by Waniganayake et al. (2000) in their research. Maybe that reluctance translates itself into the avoidance of dealing with conflict until there is no way of avoiding it.

Employment law firm Peninsula conducted a study that found an increasing number of people were losing their temper in the workplace. Eight out of 10 people (79%) suffered from work rage and 91% said what frustrated them was colleagues failing to pull their weight. In addition, 71% said that verbal abuse and yelling was commonplace where they worked. Contributing factors to work rage were disrespectful behaviour from colleagues and/or management and stress at work. Other research examining the impact of morale on the work environment also found that many senior managers failed to create a high-performance working climate and the consequence caused a de-motivating climate for staff.

There is no doubt that dealing with any form of conflict is complicated and generally requires a two-pronged response. The first is to respond by using effective problem-solving and decision-making techniques. The second is to have preventative systems and this involves creating a non-threatening, risk-taking environment and having effective policies and procedures, such as complaints procedures, disciplinary and grievance policies, in place to help you respond when necessary.

The disciplinary policy is very useful when dealing with poor performance, which may include conflict and negative attitudes. Using the policy often has a positive effect, because it means the problem is identified and therefore has to be addressed. It is a good route to helping someone get back on track. It also gives the rest of the staff team the message that you are not afraid to deal with conflict. Don't be afraid to use the disciplinary policy; just get some HR advice from an independent source. It can be money well spent to seek advice, either directly or through an annual membership of a national organisation with a free HR helpline as part of the package. Do not let the fear of a tribunal get in the way of you dealing with conflict.

Preventing conflict

Prevention is better than cure, and avoiding conflict in the workplace is more likely if leaders create an atmosphere in which people feel appreciated and believe themselves to be an essential part of the organisation. Generally, treat people with dignity and respect. Build relationships and get to know people. Do it your way; but inviting people in for a cup of tea, visiting and being visible and remembering special facts about people gives you a heads up. People are impressed when you take time to get to know them. Also, staff need to feel confident that, if an ugly situation were to arise, you, as the leader, would either intervene or provide support. Many staff have to endure aggressive behaviour from parents because the leader will not do anything about it, and this gives some people the feeling they can demand anything and no one will challenge them.

Back your staff. If necessary have a code of conduct displayed. Some people I have met have simply never been sensibly challenged and think the only way they will get heard is if they shout and demand. They also know that most people working in early years are child-focused and would not want a child to be excluded because of bad parental behaviour.

I think this needs to be dealt with and I will not tolerate aggressive behaviour at all. I will call the police if necessary; but, funnily enough, when people see you are not going to be backed into a corner they calm down and you can move on from there. Children see enough aggression outside the nursery; the one place they should expect to see adults behaving in an adult way is in their early years setting. Most early years parents are also quite child-focused and also would not want their child to be excluded because of their own bad behaviour. The majority are sadly just used to behaving in a particular way and it takes a bit of time to change.

Staff need to be encouraged to consider themselves as excellent reflective practitioners, and leaders need to continually take every opportunity to generate excitement over what staff have achieved and what challenges must be met for the future.

Leaders who give new ideas careful thought and consideration are more likely to reduce dissatisfaction and conflict in the setting. We are not as good at praise and encouragement as we like to think and I am often surprised when an agency staff member gives you a long look when you say 'Thank you for today, it's been great having you here'. We tend to give praise only for marvellous things and take a lot for granted. We ought to praise staff the way we do the children, giving it in a measured way with a clear explanation that thanks them for their contribution. Generalised continual praise works for no one and that is not what I am recommending, as this has equally unsatisfactory outcomes ranging from arrogance to disregard.

Another way of reducing the chances of conflict at work is to read the signs. If you have introduced a change, no matter how small, the chances of conflict are raised. This is particularly the case for early years settings when tasked with transforming children's services both within the service and in the surrounding environment. Leaders then need to instigate a programme of transformational change that is inclusive and facilitative and operating from a clear value base. Leaders need to be able to articulate the rationale, benefits and impacts of change for individuals, the local authority and partners. Specific changes will often be determined by users, so leaders need to build a high level of responsiveness into the service and to make sure that the pace of change is acceptable to users.

Given this huge agenda it is important to be able to manage those staff who respond by being confrontational and create a very unpleasant atmosphere when they are given new tasks or expected to adapt work practices. Usually, it is because they are worried that new projects mean more work and they may not be able to do it. Their fear of failure may be quite rational as they may be worried that their lack of competence will be judged against them and they will lose face, status, reputation or, ultimately, their job. So, another means of reducing conflict in the workplace is to create a non-blame organisational ethos, where risk taking is allowed and mistakes are treated as learning experiences. This helps build an atmosphere of openness and responsiveness where people's spontaneity and originality are respected.

Leaders need to use their emotional intelligence, which can be described, on the one hand, as being sufficiently self-aware, to be able to recognise their own emotions and manage and control them, given the impact these emotions can have on relationships in the workplace. On the other hand, as ABBA sing, 'Knowing me, knowing you' is pretty critical, as emotionally intelligent adults also operate a social awareness by being able to sense other people's emotions, see the world from their perspective and take an active interest in their concerns. It is important for leaders to apply their social skills to take charge and inspire and lead the future.

Gossip and the grapevine

Sometimes we can be a bit pious in early years and think we are far too nice to go in for office politics. The truth is, there are politics everywhere and leaders are often the last to know what is really going on. Sometimes it is because leaders are protected by people who make it their business not to let them hear the gossip, or leaders may not be around enough to hear the gossip over a chat at the photocopier. However, office politics, also known as 'the grapevine', are often a source of conflict and bad feeling. Much of this is power-playing, with staff jostling for attention.

The world will never be free of gossip, as people like a little scandal, and gossip can do this, but it must be managed. Keep a rein on it, so it does not lead to bullying but has the cachet of a sneaky look at *Hello!* while in the hairdressers. Do this by walking around, being visible and being human.

Managing conflict

Conflict can cause stress, especially if it is something that smoulders for a long time and is not easily resolved. Dealing with a destructive staff member takes a long time because of the requirements of Employment Law and leaders have to try and manage this. Very often you have no one to talk to in work as you do not want to burden your staff or look unprofessional. Having a mentor is useful for this and many other situations where you need a neutral shoulder to cry on.

Negative stress (some stress is good) is about how we respond to the situation and it can become physical. Symptoms such as sleeplessness and difficulty getting to sleep, fidgeting, dizzy spells, nausea, irritability, difficulty relaxing and concentrating are associated with stress, although these are also symptoms of a range of minor and major ailments. It makes sense to check or seek advice for symptoms, because they can be a sign that something is wrong with the body.

Recent research at Warwick University found that stress at work was closely linked to job satisfaction. It was found that there has been a steady rise in stress in the workplace since 1993 and stress was generally linked to continual uncertainty about what was expected of staff and the demands for more and more work at higher and higher standards with fewer and fewer resources. Staff in the early years sector would recognise this, given the continuing external demands from legislative changes and the increase in inspection and target-based services delivery. Interestingly, staff across all sectors agreed their job satisfaction came not from higher pay but from happy and positive working conditions, good supportive management and lots of training and development opportunities.

Top tips

Remember: when dealing with an aggressive adult, the best outcome is to resolve the situation. The following tips are useful. Try to:

- Stay calm

- Avoid showing fear

- Give them some personal space

- Understand the amygdala hijack (see page 60)

- Read the body language (much aggression is posturing). Copy their movements and then they will start to copy yours and in that way you move them into a less aggressive pose quite unconsciously. It works but you have to be calm to remember to do it

- Put yourself in their shoes; think what would calm them. What kind of service do they expect? (They often have a point, or it may be there has been a misunderstanding)

- Avoid patronising them or getting on your high horse. Give them a chance to calm down. It is amazing how easy it is to sound judgmental without realising it

- Actively listen to them (it is surprising how many people get cross because they have been passed from pillar to post and all they want is someone to listen and take them seriously)

- Ask questions, but not too many. Balance talking and listening. Hear what people are saying even if you do not like it or agree with it. Allow people to explain their behaviour or performance and to suggest mitigating circumstances

- Recognise your own attitudes and how they might be impacting on progress. Try to see other peoples' points of view

- Aim to resolve the difficulty through negotiation and understanding. Find ways of letting people know that you are acknowledging and being sensitive to their feelings. Look at the issue from both perspectives and find a compromise

- Encourage people to suggest solutions and a way forward. Involve them in designing changes to the service

- Be clear about your own values. Have a bottom line. When you are clear you are less likely to sound defensive. For example, 'I am happy to listen but not if you shout at me'

- Ensure your policies and procedures back up your decision or stance

- Get in touch with yourself and reflect. Did you make things worse? Was their point well made?

- Have you lost sight of the ethos? Has the setting become less open to new ideas?

- Have a post mortem. Talk to staff, examine the issues. What can be learned? Try asking the five Ws: Who, What, When, Where, Why

- Have a follow-up meeting to ensure that the compromise or solution is working for everyone. Agree a review period and make clear what will happen at your end to solve the problem; but remind them that another similar outburst would not be acceptable and explain the consequences

- In some instances, write up and give a contract to people. Ask them to sign to say they agree that it as a fair recording of the meeting and the outcome.

Stress

Some stress is good for you but too much stress can damage your health. Finding strategies to manage stress is the most successful approach. What are your stress management strategies? Answer the following questions and use the answers to help you to make a plan. Do you:

- Look after yourself?

- Start the day relaxed?

- Give yourself breakfast?

- Keep a check on caffeine and alcohol levels?

- Take enough exercise?

- Eating the right foods?

- Take proper breaks? Go out to lunch every now and then: call it networking

- Make sure your working environment is healthy? Do you have a comfortable chair?

- Put yourself first every now and then?

- Protect your own time? Relaxation and leisure are not treats: they are essential

- Have a massage? Hippocrates said a daily oil massage was the secret of good health and success!

- Try to identify what stresses you? Then you can make changes where possible and work realistically with what you cannot alter

- Avoid rushing around trying to do too many things at once?

- Prioritise in a way that works for you?

- Identify achievable steps and then take a small-steps approach to achieve them? Make a list in a lovely notebook and then enjoy crossing off completed tasks?
- Behave assertively, say no when necessary and take control in your working life? Don't say yes if you mean no
- Keep a sense of perspective? Don't try and be perfect and remember what you have done well
- Take your staff to dinner, every now and then, so you can talk about your problems and plan the future?

Taking a different attitude

Consider Tomlinson's (2004) reference to Cleveland's (2002) attitudes being indispensable to leading complex situations. You may need to change your attitude! He suggests you should have:

1 A lively intellectual curiosity – to consider that everything is related to everything else

2 A genuine interest in what people think – and why they think that way, which means you have to be at peace with yourself

3 A feeling that you have a special responsibility for envisioning the future – this is different from a straight-line projection of the present

4 A hunch that most risks are there not to be avoided but to be taken

5 A mindset that crises are normal – believing that tensions promising complexity are fun

6 A realisation that paranoia – and self pity – are reserved for those who do not want to be leaders

7 A sense of personal responsibility – for general outcomes of your effort

8 A quality I call 'unwarranted optimism' – some more upbeat outcome than from adding up expert advice.

(Tomlinson, 2004, p. 127)

> ### Think and reflect!
> Reality test
>
> Self-knowledge and sensitive and empathetic behaviour are critical and key areas for personal examination could be summed up in the following 20 questions.

1 Are you positive, optimistic and enthusiastic?

2 Do you know what you know?

3   How do you show you genuinely care about each child in the nursery, are aware of and empathise with their needs and understand what is important to them and their parents, families and carers?

4   How do you foster a learning culture that encourages informal, as well as formal, knowledge sharing?

5   Do you know what your staff members' learning styles are?

6   How do you check staff understanding?

7   Do you have a high level of interpersonal skills? How do you apply them?

8   How would you describe your intrapersonal skills?

9   What different approaches do you use to share knowledge and experience? Do they work?

10 How do you scaffold knowledge to bridge gaps for others?

11 Can you articulate your approach to reflective practice?

12 How do you, the children and staff learn and develop together?

13 Are you open and honest and able to communicate both the good and the bad news in a way that does not de-motivate or antagonise others?

14 Be honest: how do you avoid letting emotion sway your judgement and your ability to be objective and impartial even in difficult situations?

15 How do you manage conflict?

16 Do you investigate, probe and question, in order to get a well-informed and creative solution?

17 What systems do you use to ensure continual quality improvement?

18 How do you stay on top of current developments, trends and theories in the early years sector?

19 Do you have professional credibility?

20 Are you building links with the local community, projecting a strong image of your organisation and ensuring the setting is 'the talk of the town'?

Activities to complete at a staff team meeting or training session

These activities are provided for use at a staff team meeting or training session to provoke discussion and get the staff to think about how they would respond and what skills, knowledge and understanding they would use and why.

Activity 1

You have a new trainee member of staff. This is her first job and she seems eager to please. You have been giving her lots of praise and she has accessed quite a few training courses. However, recently you notice that she has been quite moody at times, making little eye contact, being quite brusque and especially sharp and intolerant with a certain member of staff. Staff are inclined to tiptoe around her and wait until she softens up. You are unhappy because it is causing tension and conflict in the room.

- Why are you concerned?
- What do you do?
- What policies will you use to help you?
- How do you respond to the other staff?
- How will this reflect on the employee's future?

Activity 2

You have a contract with the local authority to provide 30 places for children from the Two Year Old Programme. The places are spread between four settings. You discover at a contract meeting that one of the senior staff in the settings is refusing to take any more two year olds unless they have no additional needs and he is also asking for girls.

What decisions do you take? Explain the process for making the decisions and consider how these will support continual improvement of the setting. In answering, remember to describe:

- What information you will need (details, facts, statistics, feedback, relevant internal and external research and examples of good practice)
- Where you will get reliable and sufficient evidence for your decisions
- What challenges you envisage in getting information
- How you will check that the evidence is lawful and fits the organisational values and policies?

5 Developing the pedagogical leader

The Government's childcare strategy is based on the belief that good-quality early years education and childcare is good for all children but especially good for those who come from socially deprived and disadvantaged families and communities, and ultimately may address wider social justice issues such as poverty and community cohesion. According to David Cameron (Speech on Quality of Childhood, 2007), 'Strong families must be at the heart of our social revival.' The caveat is that low-quality childcare does more harm than good particularly for poorer children.

The challenge to early years leaders is to understand what makes childcare good quality and how to guarantee this for all children but especially to boost the life chances of children from disadvantaged backgrounds and help close the achievement gap between them and their peers. I think it is critical to get to grips with this, particularly as many early years staff are reluctant leaders and fear they will no longer spend time with children but will, instead, be consigned to the management aspects of the job. They did not imagine that creating and implementing a pedagogical vision was part of their leadership role.

Therefore this chapter considers the concept of the pedagogical leader and leaders' roles in generating the best learning environment for all children so they blossom.

> *Investing in early years is as close as it gets to magic without being magic. Parenting support and enriched day care, preferably both together create children with better behaviour and attitudes who will arrive at school with a capacity to learn.*
>
> (Sinclair, 2006, p. 49)

It is worth remembering that leadership is as much about the social context of the day as it is about the leader. The leader reflects the expectations of the day, and nowhere more obviously than through public policy; for example, the policy that says childcare needs to be a flexible and allow parents to choose the time and hours they wish their child to attend. This, in turn, places an expectation on the leader to deliver this service and meet the demands of the day. For example, today the concept of targets and performance outcomes dominate and leaders need to deliver these in a way that is appropriate.

Pedagogical leadership influences

If you stay long enough in any sector you tend to see ideas that come and go and some that get repackaged. Back in the early nineteenth century, Friedrich Froebel (1782–1852) believed that children were inherently good but could go bad due to inappropriate education. He called for the right education, which he thought could make humans perfect.

We are probably less optimistic than Froebel but the sentiment is similar: how to find a way of making life better for children so they put it to good use in the future. Blatchford (2008) noted that in most of the effective settings, better leadership was characterised by a clear vision, especially when the pedagogy and curriculum were shared by everyone working within the setting. These philosophies varied from being strongly educational to strongly social or a mixture of both, but all were very child-centred.

Many settings are influenced by the theories of Reggio Emilia (Italy), Maria Montessori (1870–1952), High Scope (America) and Te Wh¯ariki (New Zealand). However, all settings in England operate within the four guiding principles of the Early Years Foundation Stage 2012 including :

- Every child is a unique child who is constantly learning and can be resilient, capable, confident and self-assured

- Children learn to be strong and independent through positive relationships

- Children learn and develop well in enabling environments in which their individual needs are met and where there is a positive partnership with parents

- Children develop and learn in different ways and at different rates.

For this to happen, staff need to be able to lead and develop and translate these principles consistently.

Other research, including the Ofsted (2013–2014 Annual Report), and EPPE (Effective Provision of Pre-School Education) and REPEY (Researching Effective Pedagogy in the Early Years) reports in 2004, also shows that it is the delivery of integrated care and education, led by competent and stable leaders with a good understanding of appropriate pedagogical content that makes a big difference to children's successful learning and ultimately to their life chances. In the words of the very wise New Zealand curriculum Te Whāriki, all children should be helped:

> ... to grow up as competent and confident learners and communicators, healthy in mind, body, and spirit, secure in their sense of belonging and in the knowledge that they make a valued contribution to society.
>
> (Te Whāriki, 1996, p.9)

Throughout this book, I have noted that successful leaders know their sector. Gone are the days when you could import someone who had led an organisation on the grounds that they had leadership skills. Adair (2002) reminded us of the Socratic belief that leaders needed to acquire the appropriate technical competence and experience if they wished to lead others. The importance of understanding the leadership context and having appropriate knowledge is, therefore, considered even more important in early years than in other fields. Christopher Day is quite clear that leadership is about passion. He says it is about:

- A passion for achievement
- A passion for care
- A passion for collaboration
- A passion for commitment
- A passion for trust
- A passion for inclusivity.

(Day, 2005, p. 425–37)

Lambert (1998) said that leadership was about learning, which implied leaders needed to be capable in what they know, what they can do, their attitudes and moral purpose and their understanding of the context in which they work.

Pedagogical leadership therefore implies that the leader has to understand pedagogy. In simplistic terms, pedagogy is how the Greeks described the process of leading a child to learning. The Romans developed the term into the concept of education: the art and science of teaching. I like to think of a pedagogical leader as someone who understands how children learn and develop and makes this happen, taking account of every element of the service from home to school including significant relationships at home, at school and within the wider community.

It is crucial to remember that pedagogy can be influenced by context and research and a competent pedagogical leader needs to be able to debate new ideas and practices against preferred pedagogical principles, and have a sound understanding of children's development and experience. Sometimes the new is not the best and sometimes it is; what we need to be able to do is to examine it thoughtfully, consider our own responses and whether they are appropriate, and then choose what will advance the children's life chances. We must set goals that are aspirational and inspirational. We cannot do this if we have a limited grasp of pedagogy and we are unable to share and make explicit the pedagogical ethos of the setting so the staff can appreciate and implement it consistently.

My favourite pedagogues

I have some personal favourite pedagogues who have influenced my view as to how things should happen. For example, Johann Heinrich Pestalozzi (1746–1827), the Swiss educational reformer who is often considered to be the founder of the modern pedagogical debate including campaigning for everyone to receive a general education; although when he approached Napoleon about a national education programme, Napoleon told him he was too busy to be worried about the alphabet. One of Pestalozzi's fundamental principles was that it only becomes possible for individuals to do justice to their higher destiny and to develop their own moral life if those individuals receive an appropriate education.

The concept of what is appropriate is the basis of the pedagogical debate and those of us leading early years settings need to have had some level of debate so that we are clear why we are doing what we do and how this will look in our setting. For example, I especially like Pestalozzi's emphasis on the emotional well-being of the child through giving clear moral guidance. His three basic moral emotions were love, trust and gratitude. He talked about children learning obedience, not as a form of suppression but on the basis of freedom in that it teaches the child how to obey his own conscience, freed from his own selfishness and instincts. The aim is for a child to be willing to share with others, to help others and to do them favours. Pestalozzi placed quite an emphasis on the importance of adults giving a good example to the child and stated that trust and obedience would only develop if the educator showed trust in the child. What lives in the souls of parents and teachers sets a corresponding chord vibrating in the child's soul. Pestalozzi's belief was: 'The greatest victory a man can win is victory over himself.'

According to Pestalozzi the mother–child relationship was fundamental to the healthy development of the child. The three basic moral emotions (love, trust and gratitude) could only develop optimally in the child if the mother satisfied the child's natural needs in an atmosphere of loving security. Therefore Pestalozzi favoured the home as the true basis of any formative education and any other educational experience.

Although Pestalozzi's language is religious, which was resonant of the period, his pedagogical principles are quite modern. The translation into the personal, social and emotional curriculum may be more prosaic but fundamentally it tries to raise the issues of the child's moral well-being within a modern, secular and multicultural context. The pedagogical leader will, therefore, have to be able to decide how to make this work, because it is the basis on which a child will thrive and develop.

Many other pedagogues have added to the shaping of modern pedagogy. Froebel's educational approach was based on the principle that children learn through self-activity and play, which was not trivial but highly serious with deep and meaningful importance. He also saw the adult's role as supporting children's moral development and doing it in a way that takes account of children's developmental stages, something we learn more and more about as research gets even more advanced. He required staff to be trained because, like Pestalozzi, he saw their relationship with the child as vital. He also believed that there could be no success without linking the home to the school and there being a joint engagement in the child's education.

Another great pedagogue who has influenced my pedagogical leadership is Rudolf Steiner (1860–1925), who developed his thinking on the principle that learning integrates practical, intellectual and artistic elements and is coordinated with everyday life. He was keen on the importance of the imagination and creativity in learning. Like his predecessors, his aim was to create free, moral and intellectual young people, fit and able to fulfil their unique personal goals. He wanted an environment where cooperation took priority over competition and children learned through imitation and example. Language, which was crucial, was learned through storytelling, fairytales, music, poems and movement games. Modern Steiner schools reduce media influences as they believe they are harmful in the early years, something I would also advocate, given the growing research messages that claim that television, in particular, adversely affects young children's language, concentration and quality of play.

More modern pedagogues, such as Paulo Freire (1921–97) have explored other areas of education. His work among the poor and disadvantaged is of great interest to me, especially given the pressure on us to find ways to build a pedagogical bridge to help children from disadvantaged backgrounds. Freire's leader is a unifier of ideas and leads the beliefs in action. He suggested that the way to do this was to accept that children come to school not alone but with a whole set of skills, knowledge and experience which have been given to them from their home, kinship, history and culture. Teacher are, therefore, people who learn from their children and their community as much as the learner learns from them; thus the principle of the teacher who learns and a learner who teaches. His message is never to underestimate the power of the adult in the child's learning journey. For example, children are keen to learn but they do not necessarily discriminate, so they learn the good and the bad. This means they learn our bad habits and attitudes and copy our sloppy poor practice as quickly and as effectively as they learn from our best practice. This message resonates deeply with me, particularly when working with children already disadvantaged by poor adult role-models at home. It raises the level of responsibility for the leader to lead a positive, effective service that increases advantage.

Modern pedagogy is also very influenced by the works of psychologists such as Jean Piaget (1896–1972) and Lev Vygotsky (1896–1934) whose contributions have helped us shape the learning environment we create. Their views, based on children's development, knit many pedagogical concepts together and enable us to produce the best possible learning environment for children. Vygotsky's description of the child as an apprentice, learning and contributing to the development of their own generation's knowledge, greatly influences the way I work. I particularly like the principle that every generation stands on the shoulder of the previous one and that the new generation builds upon the knowledge of the past. This is very important as we have to support a generation of children and their parents to prepare for the world which we do not recognise, cannot imagine and is changing at a rapid rate. I believe that this must be one of our pedagogical principles which sets the pathway for us to develop an approach where we use all that we currently know combined with children's responses and ideas to create an attitude of thinking, questioning, evaluating, experimenting and testing, so that we are constantly ready and listening for the subtle and significant changes that continually take place in this unpredictable world.

Today, we generally accept as a truism that care and education are integrated and one cannot happen without the other. Therefore pedagogical leaders also need to have a view on this, especially when leading an integrated children's centre or any setting with babies and children staying full days. The debates about care are wide-ranging so as to encompass theories of attachment, and the nature–nurture debate alongside more routine issues of sleep, hygiene, diet and fresh air. I look to the work of Margaret McMillan (1860–1931) with her demand for good physical care, food and ventilation, Maria Montessori (1870–1952) with the need for a calm and ordered child-focused environment and Mia Kellmer Pringle (1920–83) and, in particular, her four principles including the need for love and security, new experiences, praise and responsibility and recognition. None of which is so different from the eloquent prose of Pestalozzi. The research of Elinor Goldschmied and Sonia Jackson (2004) has led me to reshape the resources for babies and toddlers and, in the course of so doing, enhance my understanding of observing babies' social play and how we need to create new opportunities for them to support their friendships. If I did not take my responsibility as a pedagogical leader seriously, I may not have made these improvements and perhaps would have failed some of our children.

Neuroscience and education

Research continues to influence our practice. Sometimes, we are over eager to accept all new research and it's wise to wait until there is a balance of evidence. For example, neuroscience was initially jumped on as the answer to improving cognitive development especially in disadvantaged backgrounds. We were introduced to images of shrunken brains and told that we needed to understand how we could increase synaptic connections and if we did this we could save a child from a life of under achievement. Policies were made to ensure services could support this but nowadays there is more skepticism, and other factors such as improvement of the environment, emphasis on good language and social skills, and ways to support the home learning environment are all considered to be necessary contributory factors.

Conkbayir et al. make reference to this, saying:

As with most disciplines, neuroscience is not without its critiques. Dr. John Bruer, founder of the McDonnell-Pew Program in Cognitive Neuroscience, is dubious about what he sees as the over-enthusiasm surrounding neuroscience. He identifies the potential it has to exploit anxious parents and practitioners through government policymakers manipulating conclusions from studies to suit the requirements of their particular position concerning birth to 3s (2002). As well as noting the reticence of the educational research community, he says:

> *Serious scientists, committed to applying research to improve child development, would likely be perplexed by such ill-founded recommendations and frustrated by the public's acceptance of them... At best, brain-based education is no more than a folk-theory about the brain and learning. (Bruer, 2002, p. 132)*

It is important to note here that the scepticism may well be due to the fact that conclusions from brain science are not yet being used to their fullest potential in terms of informing curricula and practice. Instead they are being used as part of advertising campaigns (advertisements for juice drinks and bread fortified with essential fatty acids to improve concentration) and patented schemes such as BrainGym. Such campaigns and products have the power to sway public opinion, and can often be misleading in their presentation – instead of being presented in a manner which is concise in its facts, and without the surrounding 'hype'.

(Conkbayir, M. and Pascal, C. *Early Childhood Theories and Contemporary Issues: An Introduction.* London: Bloomsbury, 2014)

However, we need to balance this with the potential advantages of incorporating findings from neuroscience in early years education (Johnson and Mareschal, 2001; Shonkoff and Philipps, 2000), and instead seek to make the necessary connection between the two fields, so that findings can be used to improve current provision. For example the use of neuro imaging to study brain activity. The gap between education and neuroscience (Shonkoff and Phillips, 2000), remains and consequently creates opportunities for early childhood professionals to be misinformed by oversimplified findings or findings that have been over-generalised and simplifies like the image of the shrunken brain due to chronic neglect). Such pseudo-research may lead early childhood practitioners and teachers to accept and adopt teaching methods which are informed by questionable research that does not stand up to its claims. However, key factors which are based on robust research such as improvement of the environment, emphasis on good language and social skills and ways to support the home learning environment are all supported by neuroscience. Given that, what is needed is improved dialogue between neuroscience and early childhood education (The Economic and Social Research Council, 2007). This means neuroscientists being more amenable to communicating with early childhood professionals in order to develop a clearer, practical understanding of how neuroscience can inform early childhood policy and practice. As Howard-Jones, Pickering and Diack (2007) explain:

> *It is important for educationalists and teachers along with scientists and researchers to share together what they are finding out about successful learning in this new interdisciplinary field of neuroscience and education.*

(Conkbayir, M. and Delafield-Butt, J. *Early Childhood and Neuroscience: Theory, Research and Implications for Practice.* London: Bloomsbury, 2015)

Putting pedagogy at the heart of the curriculum

For if they [leaders] are incapable or fail to articulate what education is for, they fail to be leaders, and become no more than servants of the powerful.

(Bottery, 2004, p.196)

Nowadays, these pedagogical principles are translated through a curriculum. The early years curriculum is subject to much passionate debate which I do not propose to engage in here. However, I will assert what I perceive to be the key elements of an early years curriculum to highlight the importance of pedagogical leadership. The important elements for me would include the child, the processes and structures designed around the child and the role of the adult to help extend the child while also helping the child to make sense of their world so they own it and can mould it to meet their needs. This can be written as a pedagogical statement with the right policies and learning resources designed to support the pedagogy. For example, teaching and learning strategies may be designed to be sympathetic to children's developmental stages and individual learning styles.

The concept of assessment and evaluation, including observations and differentiation, will be a key policy. The learning environment will need to be planned to reflect the pedagogical principles, including design, decor, resources and display. So often the environment is seen as something separate, and not a true reflection of the pedagogical principles in action. To make this happen you will need to ensure staff understand how you want your setting to look, what resources you want to use and the practice you expect from the staff. For example, you may choose to stock the space only with child-sized, real tools or use only fairytales and poems to extend language development or have an art area as a central space because art is at the centre of your pedagogical approach. Whatever your approach, what actually matters is that you have a clear, well-considered rationale for how you do things.

Clearly, relationships are very important to any curriculum and how you form and maintain them will flow from your pedagogical principles. So if, like Pestalozzi, you think home and school are on the same continuum you may decide to create a home learning environment with activities and a set of behaviours that will bring this to life whether it is weekend cameras, DVDs on a loop, home learning bags and other ways you deem important to connect with the family. How staff are allocated, encouraged, taught, supported and guided will also reflect your pedagogical principles, such as the Froebellian notion that how children are enabled to learn is just as important as what they learn.

The Ofsted report (2008) on early years leadership, which remains relevant, describes the best settings as demonstrating the following:

- Children are at the heart of all that happens
- Children enjoy taking part
- Children are given responsibility and develop independence
- Stimulating environments enable children to thrive safely

- Adults have a robust approach to keeping children safe

- Assessment informs planning

- Records are used extremely well to support children

- Staff are highly motivated and committed to the children and involved in continuous training and staff development

- Providers make further improvements on already outstanding practice

- Effective leaders know what they are doing well and what contributes to this. They are frank about their weaknesses and use self-evaluation to improve.

(Ofsted, 2008, p. 27)

Being frank about weakness is honourable and brave, but it is worth remembering that how you share this information about weakness is also critical. All too often, instead of being praised for having an ethos and systems that allow for reflection and debate to encourage thinking and improvement, all the external audience (be it the adviser, inspector or customer) sees or hears is the 'problem'. Think about how you share the message so that the audience understands that your ability to reflect on weaknesses in a constructive way can actually lead to better practice. Continual evaluation and reflection can become a way of operating, but we must balance the positive and negative.

Too often in early years we castigate ourselves or set ourselves up to be criticised and respond either in a defensive way or not at all. I believe that, if we create a culture of evaluation and have learned to articulate our thinking, we can respond sensibly and intelligently to criticism, both fair and unfair. We live in the world of media sound-bites so we need to be quick, clear and clever to get our message across in two minutes.

Leading the nursery towards continual evaluation

The following statements are reminders of how to create a culture of evaluation. Evaluation is known to make the service better, so use the statements as a checklist or turn them into questions and answer them with your team.

- Form a vision

- Share it with the staff and parents

- Keep effective pedagogy at the heart of what you do

- Create a place where it is right to ask questions

- Encourage staff to look for new solutions and then let them implement them and see if they work

- Reward creativity and innovation

- Get staff to think aloud

- Have lots of thinking activities at staff meetings
- Ask staff why they did what they did and give them time to respond
- Agree ways of improving knowledge, understanding, behaviour and practice and set clear targets
- Involve everyone in the process
- Set SMART (specific, measurable, achievable, recorded (or reliable and time-targeted) targets)
- Display the targets in the staffroom so everyone is aware of them
- Review the targets regularly
- Set an example by leading the team forward
- Analyse the mistakes with the staff – they are a useful learning opportunity
- Be willing to learn and improve
- Capture staff creativity and use it
- Develop new opportunities proactively
- Avoid asking anyone to do anything you would not do yourself
- Create an environment where it is safe to take a risk
- Get feedback on your own performance and accept the criticism positively
- Aim high, seek constantly to improve the nursery
- Have confidence in yourself and others
- Give praise every step of the way
- Reflect on what has gone well.

'The woven mat'

I have always liked the New Zealand curriculum Te Whāriki, 'the woven mat'. New Zealand was the first country to integrate responsibility for childcare and pre-school into its Department for Education; it then created a qualification programme that ran parallel to their schools structure, including new qualifications that formed the basis for employment in any registered childcare setting. Not only did it show that education and care were two parts of one whole but it also kicked out the age-old divide between care and education that still persists in the United Kingdom.

The New Zealand curriculum also places an emphasis on social context and communities and how early years practice can weave thoughtful action into social justice. The pedagogical principles, aims and goals of the Whāriki permeate every level of practice and public service. The aims and goals transpire from the principles of providing appropriate experiences individually, developmentally, culturally, locally and educationally and are shaped through:

- Well-being
- Belonging
- Contribution
- Communication
- Exploration.

The curriculum includes values of equality and respect for children's rights, including their rights to:

- Equitable opportunities for participation
- Opportunities to develop their personality, talents and intellectual, social and physical abilities to their fullest potential, and to develop self-reliance
- Dignity and respect for the individual
- Opportunities for rest and leisure
- Protection from physical and mental abuse or injury
- Opportunities for play as a vehicle for learning and recreation
- Affirmation of their own culture, religion and language
- Full and active participation in the community
- Access to a clean and protected natural environment.

The basis of this approach to learning offers:

- Opportunities for cooperative ventures, discussions and negotiation
- A focus on children's interests and strengths
- Links with prior learning and experiences
- Fun and enjoyment
- Learning in a meaningful context, solving problems that the children have chosen
- Ways of learning that reflect a balance between listening and watching, and discovering and creative inventing.

I find that this curriculum approach weaves together strong pedagogical principles and makes the links between care and education seamless. It also has at its heart the idea of the leaderful child (Laevers, 2004), a view of children as competent, rich in ideas, curious and sociable. If you sympathise with this view, then it will have a significant effect on how you develop teaching and learning strategies as well as the design of the learning environment.

Looking for examples of best practice

Pedagogical leaders also look outside the area for examples of best practice as this extends and sharpens thinking.

> *Teaching is a complex task... Teachers who read and talk about teaching ideas and practices can enhance the efficiency of the filter: they notice more, recognise more, and have more practices for a ready response.*
>
> (Lee et al. 2013, P. xi)

You need to use all your skills to create quality where children are at the centre of the service, gain a sense of belonging, self-worth, value and respect, independence and an ability to make sense of the world.

The London Early Years Foundation pedagogy

> *To grow up as competent and confident learners and communicators, healthy in mind, body and spirit, secure in their sense of belonging and in the knowledge that they make a valued contribution to society.*
>
> (Te Whāriki)

Introduction

THE LEYF pedagogy is the way we provide for the children and families who attend a LEYF nursery.

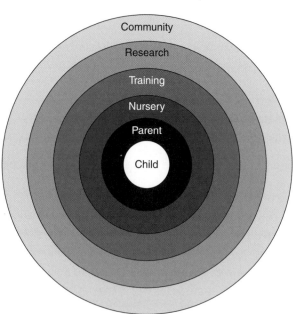

LEYF believes that care and education are inseparable. The pedagogy is holistic and incorporates everything that should be happening across the LEYF organisation. We place the child right at the heart of the service, then we wrap support for parents and staff around the child through training and research and being able to operate within the local community. The LEYF pedagogy is the means by which we make this happen and is designed to take account of children's age and stage, ability, community backgrounds, language, culture and personalities, interests and attitudes to learning. Issues such as the geography, size and shape of each nursery building are noted as this can have a complex effect on the shaping of the curriculum. The pedagogy is divided into the following areas:

- Leading for a culture of excellence
- Active research approach
- Spiral curriculum
- Enabling environments
- Harmonious relationships
- Safe, fit and healthy
- Home learning environment
- Multi-generational approach.

Leading for a culture of excellence

LEYF bases its practice on research, and the key message from the range of international research is that good leadership is key to high quality. Children need to be in a setting where high quality runs through every element of the service. This is why the first step in the LEYF pedagogy is the leadership, which is described using the LEYF framework model (see page 20). We also measure the impact we have on our children and we know that this means we have to provide children with the highest quality services. This runs through our values (inspiring, nurturing, fun and brave) – all of which are in place to ensure our leadership is driven by the values that we as an organisation have agreed are critical to a culture of excellence. Leaders are encouraged at all levels of the organisation, whether an apprentice or a member of the Central Office Team (COT) team. Everyone can begin to build each element until they are confident in all areas of the LEYF model.

At LEYF we place a high importance on creating leaders who understand empathy and emotional intelligence. Empathy is key to creative, productive and profitable organisations, and according to the Chartered Management Institute empathetic leaders are not only nicer but perform better across the board. To be empathetic, staff need to be able to identify and understand the other person's feelings, ideas and see things from the other person's perspective, whether a child, staff member or parent. We see it as listening with your heart as well as your head, and showing empathy makes you the sort of person people love working with. We believe this is an attitude that grows the kind of trust and genuine sincerity that comes when people can see and feel that you care about someone's problem. We believe that leaders who are more democratic, visionary and coach staff are far more effective than those who rely only on the command and control approach. Every LEYF manager has a part to play: leading by example, making value-based decisions and rewarding the right behaviour, not just results.

The best way to begin the leadership journey is through self-development and making best use of the LEYF Academy, which represents our organisational ethos, values learning and encourages all staff to take up training and learning opportunities at every level. The Academy is designed to:

- **Support** all staff to provide the highest quality service
- **Provide** all staff with the training they need in order to be highly effective in their role
- **Assist** all staff to gain new knowledge and skills required to meet new or changed competencies
- **Enable** all staff to attend appropriate training courses to develop their abilities and to satisfy the current and future needs of the organisation
- **Monitor** and evaluate training to ensure that it is relevant, of high quality and cost effective
- **Co-operate** in relevant research projects that will improve the service.

Personal development is also encouraged at LEYF through internal and external learning and development opportunities, mentoring and coaching opportunities, peer to peer learning and effective supervision. LEYF also prides itself on its high quality apprentice programme, which supports many young people in the development of a childcare career.

LEYF is a learning organisation where staff have the power to roll out new ideas and practice through our action research approach. A learning organisation has a common understanding of its aims and ways of working which are powerfully embedded through a shared commitment to learn together through action research, reflection, critical quest and professional development.

Action research approach

In reality, this means: *If you want to learn something, teach it to someone... by talking it out we clarify an issue in our own minds.*

Practitioner research is, as the name suggests, research carried out by practitioners, but importantly it is 'for the purpose of advancing *their own* practice' (McLeod 1999). Pascal and Bertram (2002) talk about the importance of involving practitioners in the delivery of a service not just trying out something new but instead deeply questioning 'why', 'what' and 'how' things are done. We believe that when practitioners get involved in systemically gathering evidence to gain a greater knowledge of their own impact on the services it builds their confidence and understanding to make constructive changes for the better.

David Kolb's (1984) idea that you can continue to acquire new knowledge by getting the idea and the theory and making sense of them through real experiences is fantastic. Our 'Each one teach one' programme is an example of how we train staff to cascade our LEYF approach using pedagogical conversations and developing technology skills by testing the recording of this learning using a tablet. This is one way learners can strive for an ever-greater balance between themselves and an increasingly complex environment. In searching for the answers they open up new ways of thinking, more learning experiences and greater degrees of initiative and responsibility.

Spiral curriculum

The best preparation for being a happy and useful man or woman is to live fully as a child.

(Plowden Report 1967, pg. 188)

The LEYF curriculum is described as a spiral because the role of the adult is to intertwine with the child and the environment to shape and extend their capabilities, needs and interests in order to introduce, enhance and embed new knowledge, skills and understanding. This can mean creating many spirals around the child.

All areas of learning and development are important and inter-connected. However, in the EYFS, three areas are particularly crucial for igniting children's curiosity and enthusiasm for learning, and for building their capacity to learn, form relationships and thrive. These three areas, known as the prime areas are:

- Communication and language
- Physical development
- Personal, social and emotional development.

Providers must also support children in four specific areas, through which the three prime areas are strengthened and applied. The specific areas are:

- Literacy
- Mathematics
- Understanding the world
- Expressive arts and design.

These statutory requirements are built into the LEYF pedagogy and will be strongly evidenced if staff apply the LEYF approach in all the learning areas.

How children are enabled to learn is just as important as what they learn. The LEYF approach to learning recognises the child as a competent, creative and curious being and encourages them to take responsibility for their own learning. LEYF staff are required to support children at a suitable pace, stretching and encouraging and celebrating as they move onwards on their learning adventure. This means staff must know the child and their unique ways. LEYF staff will operate a key person system which helps build a personal relationship with the child and makes it easier to help the child settle and benefit from being at nursery. All staff will get to know the child's interests, abilities and understanding in order to support and extend their learning and celebrate their achievements. LEYF staff will be sensitive to children and understand their role in helping children make friends, find their place in the nursery and value their thinking and independence.

Vygotsky describes children as an apprentice who learns and contributes to the development of their own generation's knowledge. At LEYF we translate this into supporting children's active learning and their willingness to learn from the past and their surrounding world. We offer activities and experiences which offer breadth and balance and means each child is given access to a wide variety of experiences in order to develop a range of skills and concepts, positive attitudes towards and knowledge.

We, like Froebel, believe that play is the best vehicle for children's learning and is "not trivial but highly serious with deep significance". It is vital for children's development and welfare. Play is the means by which they express strong feelings, rehearse experiences and interact socially, often with great enjoyment. Play is the main medium through which we teach and will include a daily balance between free flow and child initiated play with planned activities that engage children which will stimulate curiosity, creativity, wonder, fun, enthusiasm and enjoyment. Learning is active, fun, sensory and hands-on and a central role for LEYF staff is to provide support, encouragement, warmth, acceptance and challenges for creative and complex learning and thinking.

LEYF staff are taught to help the children scaffold their learning, using a range of different but appropriate teaching strategies including conversation, listening, observing, modelling, questioning, discovering and creative inventing. The quality of interaction is critical as well as the quality and sensitivity of the intervention. Scaffolding and differentiation together help children to become independent learners. It is also encouraged when children learn from each other. Encouraging situations within LEYF nursery routines where children of similar competence play together. The LEYF buddy system is another means of scaffolding led by the children where more competent and knowledgeable children help others to reach a higher level.

LEYF believes that celebrating and making children familiar and comfortable with their family heritage and the predominant London cultures actively supports their self esteem, makes them more confident and open people and thereby contributes towards countering racism and racial prejudice. We also believe that children need to share their experiences with friends from many social and cultural backgrounds as early as possible as it has a significant impact on how they view themselves and their relationship with the world. Children exposed to organisations like LEYF, which has as its heart inclusivity, equitable opportunities for participation and diversity, have been shown to cope better with difference, preparing them better for their role in a globally connected world.

At LEYF we value local cultural and community experiences and we build on this. Children are taken out weekly to shops, cafes, local amenities and elderly people's homes. We visit the local art galleries and museums on a very regular basis. We also work with the education departments of some of the large national institutions such as the National Ballet, Tate Britain, Tate Modern, Wigmore Hall and the Royal Philharmonic Orchestra. This is in addition to getting involved in a range of local events and activities, from library visits and local walks to attending local food and art festivals.

During the week, children at LEYF will conduct their own planning meetings to ensure their voices are heard and that staff are familiar with their interests. Children should have control over their own learning and play a role in learning how to learn and think about things. Like Montessori, we consider the importance of the "absorbent mind," and the limitless motivation of the young child to achieve competence over their environment and to perfect their skills and understanding. Planning led by children is one way of doing this, and these weekly meetings are supported by daily adult-planned activities to provide differentiated and extended learning activities. Children will use Makaton throughout the day with the key 20 words/symbols as the basis of all Makaton interaction, as a means of supporting their ability to communicate.

To be able to assess children, staff are expected to recognise and note the gap between what a child can do and what is needed to take them onto the next level of learning. The first stage of this is through observations, and then staff can scaffold the child's learning and build in activities using LEYF planning systems to help the children grasp the next level of learning.

At LEYF, planning is a dynamic process, which involves a continual cycle of planning, observation, evaluation and recording. Planning is most effective when it gives staff clear guidance as to how to meet the needs of the children. Planning needs to be flexible so as to take account of children's developmental stages, needs, ideas but also allow learning to develop spontaneously. Children pass through developmental stages but will also be continually moving backwards and forwards along the developmental continuum. Children learn best in their own way at their own pace.

Planning needs to be thoughtful and appropriate and a joint team effort where ideas and experiences are brought together to effectively contribute to the service provided to the children. Planning will always be enhanced if parents are informed and involved. Parents will be given the opportunity to add their comments to 'learning journeys' as well as being able to fully discuss their child's progress at termly parents' evenings.

Children are offered their own opportunity to assess the nursery through their 'exit interviews', which help us see the nursery from their perspective and then make the necessary amendments.

Enabling environments

Most LEYF nurseries are kept small (despite the costs), and will always be sited right at the heart of the community. The environment must be a place of beauty and order. At LEYF, we believe that the context of learning includes all aspects of the environment: the living, the physical, and the material worlds. Our job is to enable children to explore and make sense of the world. Like Montessori, we want to provide a stimulating, child-oriented environment that children can explore, touch, and learn from without fear.

Every LEYF nursery conforms to a particular decoration and design pattern. We believe that children deserve the right to be educated in appealing and attractive environments. We took account of the views of many which were best summed up by Goldschmied and Jackson (2004), who commented that many environments offered to young children were often ill-thought out and ugly and not designed from a pedagogical leadership perspective. LEYF has ensured that our design approach offers the children the best environment in which they can learn and develop.

Like Montessori, we believe that "environment" includes not only the space the children use and the furnishings and materials within that space, but also the adults and the children who share their days with each other. Montessori believed that the teacher has a responsibility to provide wonderful sights, textures, sounds, and smells for children. She also believed that part of sensory experience for children is having tools and utensils that fit their small hands, and tables and chairs that match their small bodies. Beautiful, orderly, child-sized environments and sensory play are part of Montessori's legacy.

Every LEYF nursery is a different shape and size, but all are/have:

- A cream, blue and white colour scheme
- Good lighting
- Hessian display boards
- Wood and wicker (limited plastic)
- Uncluttered, clean, well-ordered
- Neutral, calm, quiet and homely
- Low on tables and high on floor space
- Accessible low level units organised so children can find and put away what they need
- Natural materials
- Rugs, cushions, sofas
- Sensory materials and activities
- Vegetables and real food in the role play area
- Real tools that work (sharp knives, good scissors, woodworking and cleaning tools)
- Dens and quiet spaces

- Communication-rich in all areas

- Urban outdoors.

One of the fundamental purposes of LEYF nurseries is to ensure that we have ambitions for all children but especially those from poorer families. We know that the difference between children from professional families and those who experience disadvantage is the richness and variety of language.

> Literacy unlocks the door to learning throughout life, is essential to development and health, and opens the way for democratic participation and active participation and active citizenship.
>
> (Kofi Annan, Ghanian diplomat, UN Secretary-General 1997-2006)

In early childhood, one of the major cultural tasks for children is to develop competence in and understanding of language. Language does not consist only of words, sentences, and stories. It also incorporates art, dance, drama (including pretend play), mathematics, movements, rhythm, and music. Children are learning to communicate their experience in many ways and to understand the ways in which others have communicated and represented experience. They are developing increasing competence in symbolic, abstract, imaginative and creative thinking. Language develops in meaningful contexts, when children have a need to know and a reason to communicate. Adults will need to understand and respect both verbal and non-verbal communication styles. All LEYF nurseries use Makaton and will have a display with the key 20 symbols.

The urban outdoors sums up the way we can provide children with as much freedom to play outside as possible. Children need to be supported to develop a respectful relationship with the natural environment. Children who display curiosity about their environment and able to explore, experiment, discover, interpret and evaluate their findings are more likely to continue to engage in these learning processes throughout life.

LEYF staff are therefore expected to:

- Be passionate about nature and the environment

- Champion outdoors play

- Be out in all weathers

- Wear suitable clothing

- Teach the children to stay healthy

- Allow the children to take risks

- Build a mud kitchen

- Build a fire pit and cook outdoors

- Recycle and use recycled materials

- Grow plants, herbs and vegetables from window boxes to allotments

- Explore local community spaces through daily local walks and outings.

Harmonious relationships

At LEYF, we believe that harmonious relationships promote children's wellbeing and help them to grow up as strong and independent people. Children who are nurtured by adults learn to form, develop and sustain positive, harmonious and empathetic relationships. Sensitive, tuned-in adults support children's learning by the warmth and encouragement of their responses.

The LEYF adult is best described as 'tuned in', which means that staff:

- Apply strong child development knowledge
- Know how children learn
- Sustain sensitive and positive relationships with everyone
- Help children to know they are lovable and valuable
- Understand children's personalities and idiosyncrasies
- Can scaffold and extend learning, always one step ahead
- Enjoy being with the children and have lots of fun
- Create the right environment
- Are great conversationalists
- Understand children's emotions and can calm and reassure them
- Understand attachment and impact this has on children
- Listen carefully to children so they know they are heard and understood
- Involve them appropriately in discussions and decisions such as planning meetings, feedback projects and exit interviews
- Provide appropriate help as soon as possible so children learn to feel safe
- Support children to problem-solving
- Understand and are able to put into words to feelings and learn to regulate emotions and reason solutions to problems
- Help children learn that their distress and discomfort does not last forever so they can gradually learn to manage these
- Are always reflecting and thinking of how to make improvements.

The LEYF Routine

A LEYF nursery should be like a home: a secure and safe place where each person is entitled to respect and the best of care. This feeling of belonging contributes to inner well-being, security, and identity.

The routine is organised to give the children structure and order in the day so that they can weave free play throughout the day, while also having access to a balance of child led and adult led activities. There is a strong emphasis on helping the children to become confident and independent in their relationships with children and adults and in how they use the nursery resources. Each child's personal, social, and emotional welfare is of paramount importance, as we believe that an unhappy or dissatisfied child will find it hard to learn and blossom. Consequently, praise and encouragement is a permanent trait of every LEYF nursery.

To help children become independent each nursery has a visual timetable and children need to understand how the day operates so they are safe and secure. Independence is also encouraged by teaching a child practical life skills through the routine, such as helping them learn to dress themselves, prepare and share meals, put their toys and clothes away and take an active part of their nursery and their neighbourhood.

Children vary in their rate and timing of their growth and development and in their capacity to learn new things in new places. They learn best in their own way at their own pace and the routine is designed to enable this to happen. Repetition of activities is integral to this learning process and children will be encouraged to repeat activities as often as they wish until they tire of them. Doing this is more likely to foster the child's natural joy of learning.

Throughout the nursery day, staff continually observe the children and sensitively intervene to support and extend their learning, using a range of teaching methods. They make every effort to recognise and bolster the children's interests so as to build their ability to concentrate and persevere appropriately. Staff also work very closely with parents who are constant in their shared interest and commitment to both their child and the nursery.

We use the systems to check that our efforts to meet the needs of the children are successful and reflect the original learning objectives.

Safe, fit and healthy

Children need to feel safe in the nursery, but this should not negatively curb their enthusiasm, curiosity or sense of spirit. Correct use of risk assessments to mitigate the risk is the means by which we balance child development, children's wellbeing and safety.

Keeping children fit and healthy requires LEYF staff to understand how to do this from hand washing to food education, activities and physical fitness.

Eating habits are developed from a young age and messages about healthy lifestyles need to be delivered in a clear and consistent manner if children are to develop the knowledge, understanding and skills they need to develop positive attitudes to diet and health. Food is a vital ingredient for the wellbeing of the children and plays an important part in the day-to-day routine in our nurseries. Where possible, the kitchen is centrally positioned in the nursery, through a hatch where the children and their parents can see the chef preparing the food. This gives children good opportunities to learn about food and creates a relaxed and trusting relationship with the parents.

LEYF believes that they should eat a healthy, well-balanced diet with varied menus using fresh seasonal foods and simple ingredients bought locally. Chefs are expected to provide high-quality meals which the children enjoy and with very little waste.

Children with allergies and food intolerances will be served food as close as possible to the ingredients used in the main meals. Chefs seek advice from the child's parents, the nursery manager and the child's key person. Information about allergies will be displayed in the kitchen as well as logged in the child's admission form. Similar information is kept about staff allergies.

Mealtimes are particularly important at LEYF and children are taught to learn to eat correctly, using good table manners so they can be confident in any type of environment from restaurant to school canteen. LEYF staff need to model good manners including sitting with the children, correct use of cutlery and socially sensitive behaviour at the table. Mealtimes are a pleasant and family-type experience, with staff and children enjoying conversations in a calm and friendly environment.

The presentation of food is very important. The table must be set with table cloths and napkins. Food is served in serving dishes. The importance of setting the table, allowing children independence to serve and the provision of those children who are servers with an apron is very important. Each child needs a placemat and those with allergies need to be able to indicate this on their placemats.

In addition to their breakfast and lunch we need to ensure that children have access to water throughout the day and where possible they have a daily intake of five pieces of fruit and/or vegetables.

The role of the LEYF chef is also very important, as the chef is expected to support the education of children and staff about food in order to reduce the increasing child obesity and poor fitness of children. One in five children under five years old, is obese with the possibility of a lifetime of illness as a result. LEYF chefs will be provided with training on a regular basis and where possible will be invited to complete the Cache Level 2 Diploma in Food Production and Cooking for Chefs in the Early Years.

Home learning environment

Of course, educating children is not simply for professional practitioners – parents have a key role. The EPPE report confirms that the home learning environment has a greater influence on a child's intellectual and social development than parental occupation, education or income. What parents do is more important than who they are, and a home learning environment that is supportive of learning can counteract the effects of disadvantage in the early years. Roulstone et al. (2011) confirmed that children's home communication environments influence their language development. The number of books available to the child, frequency of visits to the library, whether parents are teaching a range of activities, the number of toys available and attendance at pre-school are all important predictors of children's vocabulary at two years. Children's understanding and use of language at the age of two predicts how well they will perform on school entry assessments including reading, writing and maths.

In addition to family activities, 'ideas to do at home' sheets, contribution to learning journeys and termly parent's evenings, we approach HLE in three ways.

Firstly, we encourage sharing learning progress through our daily pedagogical conversations which shows parents how everyday domestic activities can have a great educational benefit. Staff are expected to be sensitive and empathetic in how they approach, manage and sustain these conversations. They need to know how to choose the best moment, how to arouse interest and to read a person's response; for example, recognising when a parent has lost the thread of the conversation and when it needs to be explained again. This requires real emotional intelligence so that parents are not uncomfortable or do not feel guilty for not being fully engaged in the conversation, whether it's because they do not want to seem impolite, look silly, don't know how to tell you that they have something else to attend, or whether they just have a lot to do.

In summary, LEYF staff need to be able to use the pedagogical conversation to:

- Understand what the children are learning
- Be able to use the information to translate the learning at home
- Motivate and encourage the child at home
- Give models that can be imitated
- Simplify the ideas into workable home activities
- Highlight the significant elements of the task
- Help parent scaffold the children's learning.

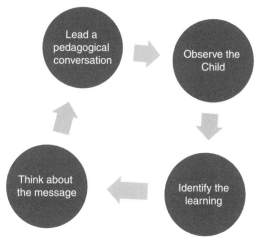

Using pedagogical conversation in an early years setting

Secondly, we have a HLE set of take home activities and finally we have the LEYF approach to reading with dialogic reading guidance for every parent. Dialogic reading is a very successful and easily understood set of techniques which have been shown to help children use more words, speak in longer sentences, score higher on vocabulary tests and demonstrate overall improvement in expressive language skills and become successful readers. In effect, adults and children have a conversation about a book.

Given the significance of dialogic reading, it is imperative that LEYF staff learn and use the dialogic reading approach, which in summary asks staff to:

- Look at the cover of the book: what can we see?
- Introduce the author, narrator and illustrator
- Open the book and look inside
- Make the link between pictures and words
- 'What do you think is next?'
- Identify the words
- 'Can anyone find another page with that word on?'
- Guess a new word using a cue from the context
- Understand the meaning of the story – both context and how we read it
- Use the dialogic prompts to get child to say something about the book
- 'Wh' prompts: Begin with 'what', 'where', 'when', 'why' and 'how' questions; these teach children new vocabulary
- Evaluate the child's response
- Expand the child's response by rephrasing and adding information to it
- Repeat the prompt to make sure the child has learned from the expansion
- Completion prompt: leave a blank at the end of a sentence using an upward inflection of your voice and get the child to fill it in. Add a familiar rhyme here; for example, you might say: "I think I'd be a commuter train. Carrying passengers here and _____," letting the child fill in the blank with the word 'there'
- Keep it light and keep it fun.

Multi-generational approach

There is no doubt about the importance of multi-generational practice to the social context of the UK and the benefits to children in early years as strong family makes strong community. Multigenerational practice can be defined as assisting individuals, families, and communities within the context of cross-generational relations and larger social systems to promote change which strengthens the inherent capacities of the family system and supports the best possible relationship between individuals and families and their environment.

(Fredriksen-Goldsen, Karen, Robin and Nancy, 2006)

At LEYF we believe that nurseries are an essential part of the community, and we ensure that the experiences, family background, interests, abilities and cultural heritage are positively celebrated and reflected across the service. A nursery represents a social world that is clearly differentiated from the social worlds of home or school. However, by building positive ongoing relationships within the local community, we can help children to recognise their role in wider society by promoting a sense of belonging and an understanding of our responsibility towards others.

LEYF is lucky to be based in London, where we can access and make best use of local cultural centres and attractions. LEYF recognises and sees the importance and value of what children can gain from understanding and being part of the richness and diversity of living in London, as well as a shared respect for their home culture of which there are 100 different cultures and languages alive at LEYF nurseries at any one time.

LEYF believes that celebrating and making children familiar and comfortable with their family heritage and the predominant London cultures actively supports their self-esteem, makes them more confident and open people and thereby contributes towards countering racism and racial prejudice.

All LEYF nurseries will have a multi-generational plan which includes the following selection of activities:

- Teen and Toddlers (a project helping young people avoid becoming teenage parents)
- Parents workshops
- Grandparents visit
- After school play club
- Elders reading stories
- Teens showing elders how to use the phone
- Tea parties across the generations
- Family picnic
- Open days for families
- South West Fest
- Barking and Dagenham Show
- Local walkabouts
- Local walks past the homes where older people live to stop and have regular chats
- Holiday to Paddington Farm with families
- International Day for the wider community
- Arts project with older children
- Partner with local elderly homes
- Contributing towards local food banks and homeless shelters
- Contributing towards children in disadvantaged countries

- Carol singing to the elderly
- Community Christmas events.

The LEYF multi-generational model places significant value on children being able to connect with the wider community, nurture extended kinship, become familiar with their neighbourhood and develop a positive attitude to forming relationships with adults of all ages. Multi-generational practice promotes health, development, and equality across multiple generations through interdisciplinary practice, education, research and community-based partnerships.

Making it happen

Kagan and Hallmark (2001) described pedagogical leadership as forming a bridge between research and practice by disseminating new information and shaping agendas. I like this approach because I think the ability to consider, cogitate and reflect on our daily practice is what ensures we keep the children and families at the heart of what we do. Pedagogical leaders need to inspire and shape a learning organisation where staff are supported and developed in such a way as to become reflective practitioners and action researchers; this contributes to a continued high-quality service. This means asking questions, listening to the answers and evaluating and changing behaviour so as to continually improve the service. This is the basis of action research, which as a process contributes to ensuring high-quality services are developed and maintained. It is a process that offers the chance to think about what we do and how we do it. It is means of taking control of practice and in doing so reducing the chances of repeating poor or ineffective practice and increasing the opportunities to improve and respond positively and to enrich the service through thoughtful, helpful and intelligent behaviour. Research is the basis of quality as it offers the chance to listen and think; until we do that we repeat what we know and we fail to hear what children are telling us.

Think and reflect!

The questions below sum up the tasks of the pedagogical leader. Use them as a personal checklist or answer them with your team.

Do you:

- Take your role seriously?
- Have excellent knowledge of how children learn and develop?

- See the world from a child's point of view?
- Communicate good practice in every way?
- Learn by teaching; teach to learn?
- Listen empathetically?
- Communicate continuously?
- Value your team and play fair with them?
- Delegate rather than dumping?
- Look after your staff and support them to reach their personal best?
- Involve the right people in the design and improvement of the service?
- Keep learning, keep reading, keep thinking?
- Think, think, think?

Children learn best

The critical factor which needs to underpin whatever you do in your setting is to remember that children learn best when they are:

- Having fun
- Excited, enthusiastic, enthralled, passionate and motivated
- Exploring, experimenting, inventing, discovering, deducing and making sense in their own way and on their own terms
- Enjoying real and authentic experiences
- Engaged with material from the real world
- Positively engaged using all their senses
- Able to use their preferred learning styles
- Able to take risks
- Allowed time for sustained concentration and to consolidate their learning
- Independent but supported by warm, kind, interested adults who understand and value them and take them seriously
- Using their imagination and personal interests
- Making sense and discovering something for themselves
- Able to take up unexpected and unforeseen opportunities
- Cared for by adults who can make systematic observations and assessments of each child's achievements, interests and learning styles.

Activities to complete at a staff team meeting or training session

These activities are provided to be used at a staff team meeting or training session to provoke discussion and to get the staff to think about how they would respond and what skills, knowledge and understanding they would use and why.

Activity 1

Last week there was a big cleaning day at the nursery. The children took their chairs and toys outside and scrubbed them down with soapy water and brushes. It was a fun experience for everyone and very satisfying. However, today a father came in to complain that he does not pay fees for his children to do your cleaning.

- How will you respond?
- How will you support your staff to respond?
- What pedagogical principles will you use and why? For example, would your response be influenced by Montessori's ideas about real jobs and responsibility?
- What thinking might you do afterwards to reduce the chances of a reoccurrence of this problem?

Activity 2

A parent complains that her child is learning nothing at nursery. She is just playing and scribbling. The child is three. The mum expects that she should be writing her name, know the alphabet and be able to count.

- How do you respond?
- How will you support your staff to respond?
- What pedagogical principles will you use and why? For example, will you refer to Froebel's work on the importance of play or more recent research from Stewart Shankar?

6 Leading to involve parents

To have happy confident children is the priority of every parent and the aim of every early years leader. Creating positive and effective partnerships with parents is the best way to help this happen. This has been the basis of good-quality childcare and education for a very long time and is now also a government edict legislated through the Framework for the Assessment of Children in Need and Their Families (2000), Children Act 2004, Every Parent Matters (2007) and regulated by Ofsted through the Early Years Foundation Stage (2008–12).

The context, which in the early years is critical, was set by the Labour government back in 1997 which recognised that lack of access to childcare was a barrier to parents, especially women, going to work. The Prime Minister at the time, Tony Blair, saw work as the best way to reduce child poverty and the consequent social exclusion associated with poverty which impacted so negatively on family life and children's life chances. This is often referred to as 'narrowing the gap'. To deal with these issues and create parent and family support, childcare was placed at the heart of his economic policy.

Getting parents back to work, supporting parenting and addressing training and workless issues was considered critical to the pledge to end the enduring high levels of child poverty and the consequent social exclusion which impacted so greatly on family life and more specifically on the outcomes and experience of children and their parents.

Changing family patterns

This parenting debate has been taking place in a context of changing family patterns and economic challenges. The most common type of family in the UK in 2010 remained a married couple with or without children, although the proportion had decreased from an estimated 72.4% of all families in 2001 to 67.2% in 2011. Of all dependent children living in families, 62.0% (8.2 million) lived in a married couple family in 2011, a decrease from 68.0% (9.0 million) in 2001. The proportion living in cohabiting couple families increased from 10.1% (1.3 million) in 2001 to 14.0% (1.8 million) in 2011. Over the same time period the proportion of dependent children living in lone parent families increased from 21.9% to 24.0% (2.9 million to 3.2 million).

Some of the problems that come from such changing patterns include child poverty which damages children's experiences of childhood and harms their future life chances. However, child poverty has increased. The UNICEF Report Card 10 castigated the UK for allowing the numbers to creep up, given the initial progress which showed a fall in relative poverty up until early 2011. However, because unlike median incomes, benefits were not falling in real terms, this improvement is now reversing; current levels of relative and absolute child poverty are expected to reach 24% and 23% respectively. The Coalition Government says it is committed to ending child poverty by 2020. To meet the goals set out in the Child Poverty Act 2010, the Government needs to lift approximately 100,000 children out of poverty each year for the next ten years. The Institute for Fiscal Studies said that the UK is unlikely to meet the target of 'eradicating' child poverty in the UK by 2020 and is more likely to return to the child poverty levels of 20 years ago.

Today, 17% of children are living on less than 60% of the national average income, 27% if you take account of the housing costs. The Poverty and Exclusion Unit at Bristol University found that the proportion of families unable to afford three items deemed necessary to life in modern UK increased from 14% in 1983, to 33% in 2012. The End Child Poverty Report 2013 brings this alive when it refers to the research from Save the Children that showed the following:

- Well over half of parents in poverty (61%) say they have cut back on food, and over a quarter (26%) say they have skipped meals in the past year

- Around one in five parents in poverty (19%) say their children have to go without new shoes when they need them

- A large number of children in poverty say they are missing out on things that many other children take for granted, such as going on school trips (19%) and having a warm coat in winter (14%)

- Only one in five parents in poverty (20%) say they have not had to borrow money to pay for essentials, such as food and clothes, in the past year

- Children in single parent families are twice as likely as children in couple families to live in relative poverty, although 66% of lone parents are in work. Over four in every ten (43%) children in single parent families are poor, compared to just over two in ten (22%) of children in couple families.

- Children of teenage mothers who also become single parents have an even higher risk of growing up in poverty as their mothers are 24% more likely to have no qualifications, limiting their chances of employment. Where a child is disabled they inherit a 34% risk of living in a family on a low income.

The risk of poverty is much higher for children in couple families where only one parent works. In 2011–12, around 20% of children living in sole-earner couple families in Britain fell below the poverty line (defined as 60% of median household income before housing costs). This compares with 4% where both parents worked full-time, and 6% where one worked full-time and the other part-time. In the same year, sole-earner families accounted for nearly 30% of all families with children in poverty.

The share of sole-earner families has fallen considerably over the last half century as many more women have moved into the workforce, including large numbers of mothers with dependent children. However, around a quarter of couples with children had only one earner in 2012, equivalent to around 1.6 million families. Most of these couples had a working father and a non-working mother. Just over half of the non-working mothers had a youngest child aged below five; the likelihood of the mother not being in work fell considerably as children got older.

Child poverty is also influenced by where you live. Within Great Britain, the top ten local authorities with the highest rates of child poverty are:

- Tower Hamlets 42%

- Manchester 38%

- Middlesbrough 37%

- Derry 35%

- Belfast 34%

- Islington 34%

- Glasgow City 33%

- Liverpool 33%

- Newcastle upon Tyne 33%

- Hartlepool 33%

(Barnardos, End Child Poverty campaign: Child Poverty Map of the UK, February 2013)

Parenting as a factor in poverty

Parenting has been examined as the other significant factor which contributes to poverty and the consequent social exclusion. Over the past twenty years, a raft of research was commissioned to examine parenting and the importance of parental involvement in children's education, as well as the impact of parental attitude to the work ethic and their willingness to contribute fully to society at every level (Every Parent Matters, 2007). The parenting issue became the subject of much greater public debate including how long-term economic outcomes for poorer children could be improved through better health and academic success Interestingly, all the main political parties share the view that economic, social and family well-being are connected and that families play a key role in building happy and safe communities.

The Government's response to the research had two strands. One strand was to get parents back to work by providing training and childcare as a leverage with the ultimate intention that they would earn enough money to move out of poverty. The second strand was to provide parents with the kind of support they needed to parent their children successfully, thereby improving their life chances. They supported the concept of early intervention which was highlighted by the Graham Allen MP (2011) report which won cross party support.

The prime window for emotional development is up to 18 months, by which time the foundation has been shaped by the way in which the prime carer interacts with the child. Emotional development takes place throughout childhood, and there is a further reorganisation during early adolescence.

(Allen, 2011, *Early Intervention: The Next Steps*)

Organisations such as the OECD also supported this view:

In the early life period, interactions and experiences determine whether a child's brain architecture provides a strong or a weak foundation for their future health, well-being and development.

(OECD, 2007)

Poverty creates hurdles for parents, in terms of poor housing and space, inadequate public transport and poor nutrition, as well as personal impediments such as lack of self-esteem and low educational achievement, leading to low expectations and aspirations for parents and children. For example, the End Child Poverty campaign found that children often feel poor because they cannot do what the majority of their school friends do, such as attend activities or invite friends round for tea. Therefore, poverty does matter because it makes good family functioning harder to attain.

The Economic Social Research Centre (2008) looked at the link between poor neighbourhoods and poverty and found some factors exacerbated the situation and others helped to alleviate it. They found that bringing up children in a disadvantaged neighbourhood was a real struggle for many families, not just in terms of being economically poor but trying to rear children and help them integrate through school and play in what was often considered an unsafe degraded environment with poor infrastructure. For many children, living in poor communities affected expectations and opportunities, and the 'poverty of place' played an important part in UK disadvantage. The high level of people moving in and out of the neighbourhood was also a negative and led to feelings of insecurity of existing residents and some hostility towards the new residents. The researchers also found that many poor families did not access specialist services, despite needing them. Another factor which added to the stress of parenting was living in poor neighbourhoods with risks of children copying the anti-social behaviour of disaffected young people and spreading problem behaviours, such as substance abuse or delinquency. This often resulted in the social norm of accepting anti-social behaviour and instability.

Living on a low income in a rundown neighbourhood does not make it impossible to be the affectionate, authoritative parent of healthy, sociable children. But it does, undeniably, make it more difficult.

(Utting, 1995, p. 40)

Weatherburn and Lind (2001) found a strong association between economic stress and child neglect and argued that economic and social stress impacted on juvenile criminal behaviour by disrupting the parenting process. This led to children becoming more susceptible to anti-social influences from peers in the neighbourhood and higher levels of criminal involvement.

Belsky and Vondra (1989) believed that the skills of adequate parenting were based on a parent's own developmental history and the quality of resilience gained from that, the characteristics of the family and child and the contextual sources of stress and support. Problems increased when low-income families suffered stress, such as absence of a supportive partner, depression or drug use, and improved when families enjoyed social support from family, friends or neighbours. They called this 'a buffered system'.

Ghate and Hazel (2002) reminded us that parents have their own needs as adults, and that access to adult leisure facilities or entertainment had not generally been thought to be part of parenting, even though these experiences could greatly affect parents' lives and, by implication, their capacity to parent.

When exploring parenting styles of parents in poverty, researchers found that poorer parents were more inclined to a more 'authoritarian' (demanding and directive, but not responsive) parenting style (Hoff et al. 2002). However, research of the literature on parenting styles suggested that two sets of parents living in different social or cultural contexts could use similar parenting practices (for example, discipline their children in a similar way), but that the meaning of these practices and the outcomes for the children might differ according to context. Therefore, different parenting practices amongst lower-income parents were not necessarily the result of inadequate socialisation or deficient role-modelling but possible adaptive responses to their environment. When a combination of beneficial factors – more education, more earnings and better neighbourhoods – come together, then parenting practices and child outcomes tended to be better.

Research by Dearing et al. (2004) in the USA found that if circumstances changed and parents became poorer, the stress of poverty caused maternal depression in the first three years of children's lives. They also noted that the resulting depression was likely to result in harsher or more inconsistent parenting. The 2010 governmental report on Growing Up in Scotland (GUS) 2010 found that

By age four, children who experienced prolonged (repeated) exposure to a mother with mental health problems were particularly likely to have poor behavioural, emotional and social outcomes. At the point when they are about to start formal education, these early deficits may affect their transition to school and their subsequent development and attainment.

(The Scottish Government, 2010)

Meltzer et al. (2000) studied the prevalence of mental health problems amongst children in the UK. They found children from unskilled working-class backgrounds were three times as likely to have a mental disorder as children from professional backgrounds (14.5% compared to 5.2%). The rate for families where the parents had never worked was 21.1%. There was also a strong relationship between mental disorder amongst children and problems of stress amongst their parents.

> *Studies also identify a number of protective factors which minimise the effects of children's adjustment to a family breakdown, including competent and warm parenting, parents' good mental health, low parental conflict, cooperative parenting post separation and social support.*
> (Mooney, A., Oliver, C. and Smith, M., *Impact of Family Breakdown on Children's Well-Being*:
> Evidence Review, Thomas Coram Research Unit, Institute of Education,
> University of London, 2009)

Poverty is not the only factor which affects parenting, and parents who have a support network may succeed despite the lack of income, including an ability to motivate their children to succeed in difficult circumstances. Different levels of 'social capital' or social disorganisation will produce different sorts of parents, and this will ultimately affect outcomes for children. However, according to Ghate and Hazel (2002), it is not being poor that is the most stressful factor for parents in poor neighbourhoods but having a difficult child.

To address some of these issues the Coalition Government introduced the Two Year Old Programme where two year olds from the 40% most deprived neighbourhoods would access 15 hours of free childcare. The intention was to help balance the home with the nursery. The policy was likely to have come from ideas such as this by Tickell, 2011, who argued that:

> *Where children do not enjoy a strong home learning environment, a good quality early years setting can compensate. Such settings are characterised by skilled practitioners working with parents and carers, offering support to improve the quality of home learning, and thus helping to improve children's progress and their relationships with parents and carers. The EYFS has played a role in these improvements, with some settings using it to engage with parents and carers – for example, by completing and getting feedback on learning journeys and journals.*
> (Dame Clare Tickell, 2011)

The basis of the review was that the nursery would have to be high quality. No requirement was placed on parents or settings to link with children centres to access parenting support nor was there any push to increase language support, despite research such as that done by the Avon Longitudinal Study of Parents and Children (ALSPAC) – who confirmed that 'children's understanding and use of language at the age of two years predicts how well they perform on school entry assessments including reading, maths and writing.' (Roulstone, S. et al. 2011). However, despite the lack of consistent language support, children attending nurseries have benefitted.

> *Evidence from the two-year pilot of free childcare showed that where children attended higher quality settings, there was a positive impact on language ability, and on the parent–child relationship.*

44% of parents thought that it had helped improve their child's speech and/or English language.

Parents felt they had gained a better understanding of their children as individuals and also different child development stages. Some parents believed that their parenting skills and their relationships with their children had improved since their child had started attending the pilot setting. The ability to provide a more stimulating learning environment at home was also attributed to the experience of using the pilot setting.

(Smith, R., 2009)

The mounting evidence of the impact of parenting on outcomes for children, communities and society as a whole has raised parenting to the status of a national priority. The challenges for parents balanced against the enormous benefits of impact of parental involvement has caught the notice of politicians. Parents have a crucial influence on what their children experience and achieve. Although parents tend to underestimate their own influence, we know from research that effective parenting can protect a child from multiple disadvantages.

In early years settings the task is to find ways to enable parents to become more effectively involved with their children's learning and the design and extension of their local services. Parents say there are times in their lives when they would like more advice and support in their parenting role, but sadly not all of them get either useful information or the relevant support. As children get older parenting gets harder, especially as peer groups become very important and, in some cases and for some periods of time, will be more significant than children's own families. However, parent involvement in their child's learning can have consequences that stretch beyond that child and their family and have a positive impact on the wider community, for example a reduction in the number of ASBOs issued.

Parental involvement in children's education has the biggest impact on their achievement, which is considered one way of future proofing a child against poverty. It is crucial that this is understood given that poor educational outcomes in the UK remain more strongly associated with social background than in most other countries, and changing this is a vital part of ending the intergenerational cycle of child poverty. Government research (Desforges and Abouchaar 2003) showed that the effect of parental involvement is greater than that of the nursery or school itself and parental encouragement has a significant impact on young children's cognitive development, literacy and numeracy skills.

The Effective Preschool Primary Education 2006 (EPPE) study showed that what parents do with their children is more important than who the parents are, and where parents engaged in a range of activities with their child, higher intellectual and social/ behavioural scores resulted. Two years later, it was further confirmed that 'parent involvement in home learning activities makes an important difference to children's attainment (and social behaviour) at 3 years through to the age of 11.' (Sylva, K. et al. 2008.)

The Impact of Sure Start Local Programmes on Child Development and Family Functioning (March 2008) revealed that children who had a better home learning environment showed better social development and higher levels of positive behaviour and independence.

The findings from the Effective Provision of Pre-School Education (EPPE) project in August 2008 reinforced the importance of home learning, especially on children's mathematical achievement.

In addition, the Avon Longitudinal Study of Parents and Children (ALSPAC) study confirmed that children's home communication environments influenced their language development. The number of books available to the frequency of visits to the library, parents teaching a range of activities, the number of toys available and attendance at preschool are all important predictors of children's vocabulary at two years old. 'Children's understanding and use of language at the age of two years predicts how well they perform on school entry assessments including reading, maths and writing.' (Roulstone, S. et al. 2011.)

This has been further reinforced by the Ofsted report in 2013, which found that parenting style, parental involvement in education and the quality of the home learning environment are major factors that explain the differences between children from low-income backgrounds and their wealthier peers. Not enough is being done to support and encourage parents, but particularly for those who need the most help to secure, for their children, the benefit that the best early education and childcare can offer.

Clear leadership that is focused on education right from the start has been key to improving outcomes in the early years.

Sure Start Children's Centres

As a significant response towards addressing child poverty, Sure Start Children's Centres were launched in 1998, and 3,500 were created in various forms. Some were new buildings with nurseries attached, some were stand-alone buildings providing multi-agency services, some were attached to existing services or based in a health centre, and some were virtual and used as a signposting service to inform families of where they would find support.

The initial purpose of Sure Start Children's Centres, which has subsequently been debated over the past ten years, was that they would develop and provide the range of parenting support that would enable parents to get back into work and out of child poverty. A key feature of all children's centres, no matter what form they took, was that they ensured parents could access affordable childcare, financial and career advice and training to enable them to gain employment and move out of poverty. It was a way of tackling poverty and its associated problems, by offering a non-stigmatised universal service where it was the norm to have support services available and where the centre could be a positive and accepted hub in fractured neighbourhoods and eventually help develop community cohesion.

The Sure Start Children's Centres were run by early years leaders who needed to know about the consequences of living in poverty with its complex and far-reaching effect on children's all-round development. New services needed to be designed to suit local parents and reflect their lives, needs, interests and communities. Leaders were asked to involve parents and embed a principle of consultation and involvement, a process that is easily articulated but much harder to do successfully. Therefore, early years leaders needed to grasp the understated complexities of parental involvement, so that all future change and development of the service would thrive on the basis that the service would be underpinned by a real and comprehensive appreciation of how poverty influenced and created different parenting approaches – which in turn impacted on children's progress. They therefore needed to review the quality and shape of the curriculum so the care and education fitted the needs of the child and the influences of their home and neighbourhood.

To do this, new and existing leaders of children's centres were required to create shared ways of working that demonstrated staff understanding of how each child's development was significantly shaped by their particular experiences; and, in addition, understanding of the interaction between a series of factors including: characteristics of genetic inheritance, temperament, health problems or impairment and the effect of the culture and the physical and emotional environment in which the child is living. The consequent system for assessment across the varied services needed to be underpinned with a similar philosophy, whether through joint or parallel assessment arrangements – especially to ensure, as far as possible, that fair assessment would be based on the following values:

- Child-centred
- Rooted in child development
- Ecological in their approach
- Ensure equality of opportunity
- Involve working with children and families
- Build on strengths as well as identify difficulties
- Inter-agency in their approach to assessment and the provision of services
- A continuing process, not a single event
- Carried out in parallel with other action and providing services
- Grounded in evidence based knowledge.

(Principles Underpinning the Assessment Framework, 2000, p.33)

The Sure Start Children's Centres were to become similar to the buffered system of support described by Belsky and Vondra (1989). They suggested the need for a network of family and friends that would support parents when they needed help to keep going. In the absence of this network of family or friends, the Children's Centre could create another type of support for parents through targeted services. Children's Centres were planned and built and many teams doubled and trebled in size overnight as they reshaped and reformed, often in a new building, with a new philosophy and a new set of expectations. The principle of creating partnerships and working together to address the problems of poorly connected services was quite a challenge and still remains so.

Creating integrated services was a necessary step, as the lack of coordination between children's and adult services was considered a critical factor in the lack of support for families, which in turn had a negative impact on the well-being of the child. Finding ways to create a process of linking health and education and voluntary sectors all together to create a local, friendly, accessible and well-coordinated responsive service was difficult. Bronfenbrenner's (1979) ecological model with its emphasis on interconnecting systems was a good starting point. The idea was that socio-cultural, community, family and individual aspects all affect each other immediately, at a distance and at different levels; in essence they are a complex web of interacting and interdependent factors. Thus context was critical because the way in which the four factors collided determined the shape of the need, and therefore the design, of the service. What it meant for an early years leader was the need to recognise the systemic influence of the family and the community on the child, as that would be the foundation for the development and shaping of the service. It would also be the basis upon which what was communicated to staff and all the operational policies would be reviewed, developed and implemented.

> *Successful leaders have a strong commitment to integrated practice, have a clear vision of what is to be achieved and are willing to take some risks to achieve that vision.*
>
> (Bertram et al., 2002–3, p. 11)

Providing a local service based on the involvement of parents and local partners places a greater demand on understanding how partners operate, especially where shared process need to operate and new policies need be translated into practice, such as Family Support Panels, Common Assessment Framework assessment and lead professionals. Some of the most frustrating discussions are at meetings where no one seems to understand anyone else's perspective and the issue at stake, namely a service for a child, is lost in the politics of the process. To reduce and ultimately eliminate this, you as an early years leader need to understand how your partners operate and their philosophy towards giving the child and parents a voice in the service. Surprising as it may seem, many services and indeed some early years staff have a limited understanding of and willingness about involving children and parents in service design and delivery, which is crucial when trying to change perceptions and create a service that will engage parents and partners more effectively. The outcome for children is vital because when parents get involved and start becoming confident enough to fully utilise and possibly contribute to a service, they usually begin to fully access the services. Ultimately we may see the sort of success stories that the government saw which include poor parents getting childcare, training and employment locally and, thus, lift themselves out of financial and emotional poverty and set a new, more secure pathway for themselves and their children.

The message of giving parents a voice in your setting should continue to be repeated at every level and should form the basis of the strategy to ensure staff, and anyone else representing the service, understands and can apply the message explicitly and consistently at every level of the service and on a daily basis. It is another aspect of the role of the early years leader – in this case, as a marketer and communicator.

Another area which has continued to challenge new ways of working in partnership is the issue of funding. Getting sufficient funds to enable a ground-up service to be developed with agreement from the various partners on what that means in reality remains complicated, especially from a government which appears not to value Children Centres. This is despite evidence from the National Evaluation of Sure Start, which

> ... has demonstrated that the availability of high quality services, early years education and support through the Sure Start Programme has resulted in families in Sure Start areas experiencing better child health, parenting, home learning environments and life satisfaction than families in non-Sure Start areas.
>
> (Melhuish, E. et al. 2010)

The Children's Centre leader has always needed financial acumen and an ability to create financial systems with checks and balances as well as fundraising skills to raise specific money needed to develop a service everyone was happy with. Now, however, the demands on finding ways to sustain a service in very challenging economic times has required leaders to develop broader business skills and ways of earning money to pay for the key services.

The Sure Start Children's Centres initiative is one of the many examples which require leaders to change quickly and demonstrate the ability to be flexible, responsive and emotionally mature. Change is frightening, even when it is for the best, as it requires people to give a little of themselves and relinquish some of their power and professional confidence. The challenge continues.

Involving parents in Sure Start Centres

Involving parents in Sure Start Centres can be a challenge. Parents are not a homogenous group; some parents do not want to engage and be actively involved and are perfectly able to self-select services that interest them, irrespective of their backgrounds or their postcode. The challenge to the early years leaders in developing any early years setting is to establish who local parents are, what they want and expect, and how to find a way of getting real information from them so that services actually meet their needs. The term 'hard to reach' has been bandied about. No parent is that hard to reach, but many services are. This is a principle that needs to be embedded into any new service development. Easier said than done! Also many parents object to being told that a service is targeted at their area because it is disadvantaged (as in the case of many Sure Start Centres). I have had many comments from parents including, 'I don't want to my children to hear people say they live in a disadvantaged area. What is that going to do for them?', 'I don't want to come here if it's associated with failed parents,' 'Are all the children coming here going to be considered social services children?' and 'What is a supra-output area anyway?' However, this was also a good opportunity for me to emphasise to parents how important they were. Many of the young dads did not feel they had much to offer, yet growing research shows that fathers' interest and involvement in their children's education is strongly linked to their well-being and mental health, greater self-confidence, positive behaviour and relationships, greater educational attainment and cognitive skills.

There is much research about how to involve parents. Since the early 2000s in particular, leaders have been handed a raft of ideas and suggestions to create a collaborative and participative environment. However, as everyone in early years knows, there is no fixed formula because everything has to be designed around the local environment. This is particularly evident when leading and delivering services across different boroughs, counties and countries. The task is to take the information and make it work. Just like working with children, outcomes are unpredictable and research initiatives may recommend that certain logical things will happen but these do not happen in your setting. There will, therefore, always be a bit of 'try it and see'. This has immediate bearing on the ethos of the organisation and the kind of staff you need to grow. Leadership of early years must now include an ability to lead staff, to be confident, to support parents and ensure their continuing involvement with their children, to ensure the setting is positive, productive and makes a difference in the immediate and long term.

Many young nursery staff say that one of the areas they are most nervous about is working with families. There are many reasons for this, ranging from a lack of confidence to never getting the opportunity to learn. Many settings face daily encounters with difficult parents which clouds the impressions of staff. One continually complaining and aggressive parent can unnerve the whole team. The involvement of staff in the development of the service is, therefore, very important. If staff realise that when you say 'open access' you mean exactly that, they can prepare themselves to manage aggressive or unpredictable parents. If you say there will be rules about behaviour and a code of conduct written into the early years setting agreement, then staff can consider how they will make this happen in reality. If you say that the service is a local service and the consequences of opening your door to everyone may mean that you become a safety net for some people, then staff will need to understand what that means and how you will train and support them to manage the fine balance between parents feeling safe enough to come and unburden themselves, but contained enough to know that the setting has rules which protect the children, staff and parents themselves from out-of-control behaviour. Staff need to understand that for many parents this may be their first experience of a service which is not, from a parental perspective, designed to confuse, alienate or ignore them. Fragile families are often suspicious of anything to do with the state, and managers from organisations with a reputation of success in engaging 'hard to reach' families have stressed the importance of a collaborative approach. This means focusing on the family's needs as identified by the family and involving families wherever possible in service delivery and design, while being realistic. Leaders need to be 'humble about their own capacity to know the final answers, and to recognise that others have significant input here, not least those normally described as clients' (Bottery 2004: 194). Starting from this perspective is one step to reducing barriers and making a safe space for everyone – and that includes setting boundaries and having a code of conduct that everyone is expected to adhere to. A starting point may be having friendly staff, listening ears, and a staff team with a willingness to accept that parents living in some neighbourhoods, constantly struggling on little money as well as with myriad personal and family dynamics, can be hugely stressful. For many families, survival is testament to their resilience and ability to adapt, modify and improve their circumstances.

We know that working with parents who have may have their own problems can present enormous challenges, particularly for young and less experienced early years practitioners. Practitioners need skills and confidence to actively engage each of these groups of parents. Confident staff are more likely to readily engage with parents on a day-to-day basis by welcoming them into settings and explaining face to face what parents can do at home. Staff will need to learn to develop the casual pedagogical conversation where they become sufficiently confident to explain to parents what and how their child is learning. Critical to this are the methods necessary to make the message understood, as the purpose will be to extend experiences from home to nursery and back again. These casual pedagogical conversations could be supported by written information, home learning resource bags, apps and other ways of reaffirming the message.

Carol Vincent (1996) examined home-school relations in a small number of inner-city schools, and devised a four-way classification of parental positions with regard to practitioners, which continues to be informative. She identified four basic 'types' of parents: 'detached parents', who prefer practitioners to take full responsibility; 'independent parents', would like more involvement but lack confidence; 'supportive parents', who readily engage with suggestions and invitations; and 'irresponsible parents', who do not support their children's learning.

The EYFS Statutory Framework 2014 states:

Staff could be made aware of the importance of their relationship with parents. Traditionally, staff in childcare settings have focused their attention on the children in their care rather than on children and their parents. Therefore, there may need to be a greater acknowledgement of the importance of parents in children's early learning so that all staff become confident about working with parents to encourage early home learning.

A significant challenge for staff working with the under-threes will be the introduction of assessment for all two year olds. The statutory guidance also states:

When a child is aged between two and three, practitioners must review their progress, and provide parents and/or carers with a short written summary of their child's development in the prime areas. This progress check must identify the child's strengths, and any areas where the child's progress is less than expected. If there are significant emerging concerns, or an identified special educational need or disability, practitioners should develop a targeted plan to support the child's future learning and development involving other professionals (for example, the provider's Special Educational Needs Co-ordinator) as appropriate.

This raises important issues for those working with the under-threes, and the sensitivity needed to carry out what might possibly be 'difficult conversations' with parents, where concerns about a child's development progress may have to be initiated. This emphasises the importance of early interventions and ongoing conversations between practitioners and parents about children's learning and development. Some early years practitioners will require training in order to help them work as partners with parents in children's learning.

There are currently some concerns that Early Years staff may miss problems or, conversely, over-identify special needs. There is a risk that if the check is not conducted and communicated in an appropriate way, it could damage relations with parents and possibly put them off future engagement.

Therefore, getting the balance right between a negative, rule-bound, unfriendly place and a friendly but unsafe, unreliable and poorly managed place can be tricky. Generally, many of the more difficult parents have learned their aggressive behaviour because it was the only way to get attention and because they know no other way of communicating when they are fearful and insecure. Being clear and honest, dealing with the situation straightaway and giving people a clear and consistent message, works in the majority of cases but occasionally a parent may be excluded until they learn how to behave in the way that is expected. One boundary I would set is absolutely no shouting or aggressive behaviour where a child can hear, see or even sense it. Some other centres may have a drug and alcohol 'three strikes and you're out' rule. The best way to get agreement is by involving the parents in the rule-making. Often, they are much more draconian than you are and your role as leader involves becoming the person who helps find the route to a more reasoned and accepting approach. Whatever the situation, to gain and maintain staff respect the leader needs to be able and willing to resolve difficult situations and set standards. Both parents and staff will receive a clear message and it supports your credibility. Poor centres are those where the leader shirks dealing with difficult issues, fails to set a clear ethos for everyone, leaves staff at the mercy of unpleasant encounters and allows a negative atmosphere to build up. Not the best place for any child, especially as this may be exactly what they are experiencing at home. Good centres are places where everyone feels safe and welcomed and the services are sensitive, culturally competent and easily available. Staff are given a combination of training, information and support as well as the opportunity to practise handling different situations in a no-blame environment, which will build their confidence and help separate the personal from the professional so they learn to respond to the situation in a more objective, calm and informed way.

Offering other services to parents

The involvement and engagement of parents into services is often seen in terms of whether services are offered at different levels. However, it is down to more than this, especially when developing a service that parents want. Families differ in their capacity to take advantage of services. Bhabra and Ghate (2004) showed that families, including those commonly termed 'hard to reach', welcomed information about child development and family services. Further studies showed that parents are often the experts on the services they need but that no one has really asked them.

There is an expectation that parents can access information through the universal services (these are services which anyone should be able to access: schools, doctors surgeries, libraries and community centres, etc.) This type of information is also available in children's centres, and there is a growing expectation that these can also signpost parents to other services. The key pressure here is that, by signing up to be able to deliver an information service, it, then needs to be up to date, relevant and effective. Therefore, given the raft of information and publications produced, some leaders may decide to focus on certain aspects of information sharing and do it well, rather than try and be all things to all people. It is also worth remembering that parents do often take a while to find out what they need and the information that interests them before firstly responding to the services and secondly engaging with them. It is not a quick process and the most effective services are offered when the staff and parents have decided together what they want, and when and where they want it. Popular sessions are full to bursting point, yet some services are empty despite a raft of advertising and information. The severity and nature of the parenting issues also has an impact and it can take time to get beyond the initial presenting issues, so no amount of information will help here; it will be the development of a relationship with the service that will help these parents to become informed and engaged.

Parents benefit from access to information and advice on child development and parenting, whether through leaflets on an information stand, a well-informed receptionist, or through a web-based stand-alone information kiosk where parents can search and print off the information in the foyer of a children's' centre or at a library or in a school reception area. Some services may include a direct telephone line to the Family Information Services. Whatever is used, the point has got to be how you measure the impact to see whether it works and if the information available answers the questions asked. Often, we don't have time to monitor and examine the impact of what we are doing.

Parenting programmes are available to many parents and are seen as a means of supporting positive parenting. I am always guided by the wise words of Winnicott who relaxed a parent by saying, 'To begin with, you will be relieved to know that I am not going to tell you what to do' (Winnicott, 1987, p.15). Parenting programmes may work for some people, but are much more likely to be successful if parents have bought into the idea of attending. How these programmes are advertised is quite critical and staff need to be able to explain succinctly what the benefits will be. Parenting programmes are not cheap and anyone leading a service which offers parenting programmes needs to be very clear as to what these entail, how they are advertised and the suitability and effectiveness of the programme. They are not quite the same as offering a phone number for a universal helpline. Parenting programmes such as Triple P or Mellow Parenting may be funded as part of the local authority's strategy for family support. Evidence from the Parent Information Point pilot programme (now the Starting School Project) in schools in the UK and the Triple P programme in Australia shows that these sorts of services can increase knowledge of child development and service availability, enhance parental confidence and normalise the use of family-support facilities. Some research also found that a key factor in the effectiveness of parenting support programmes is the relationship between facilitator and users. It affects participant engagement and outcomes; getting parents involved from the outset is a significant factor for success.

Other services available to parents through children's centres may include pre-natal classes and post-natal classes, especially to help breastfeeding mothers and those experiencing some post-natal depression. Parent and child fun and learning activities are designed for parents to bring their children to play, and parents are supported to understand their children's play and development (often called 'Stay and Play drop- ins'.) Some centres also have dads' workshops. Health clinics led by midwives, health visitors, speech and language therapists, social workers, family therapists and other practitioners whose role is to support parents help their child develop might also be offered. Both international and UK evidence show us that providing high-quality social and psychological support as part of universal child and family health services can have outstanding results in terms of outcomes and long-term cost-effectiveness, particularly for families with high levels of deprivation.

At LEYF we believe that one of the best ways to start to build bridges from home to nursery is through the pedagogical conversation. Such conversations can be more powerful because these are the times when practitioners are made more aware that the child and parent share a history, context, understandings that can enlighten the nursery about the richness of the home experience. Practitioners need to understand the powerful impact of home culture and community.

> ...without conversation... the human soul is bereft. It is almost as important as food, drink, love, exercise. It is one of the great human needs. If deprived of it, we die." Educators able to initiate and sustain such dialogue require special talents, wisdom, confidence and rich education, in the best sense of the word.
>
> (Theodore Zeldin, Conversation: How talk can change our lives, p. 128)

Staff are trained to close the conversation loop, which always begins by sharing the practical elements of the child's day such as sleep, food, nappies and activities, linking these with what the child is learning and talking about how that can be extended at home. Parents are encouraged to converse freely without fear of criticism to an adult who is genuinely interested in what they have to say, whatever the topic. In the words of Bruner (1996), education is not an island but part of the continent of culture, and so all practitioners have to understand this. Children, often working class children, come from homes where parents believe the school would not value the child's home learning. For example, we noticed a child who was very knowledgeable about football. He used complex language to describe the game and was able to match players with teams and kits with aplomb. When we spoke to Dad he was bemused and had assumed we would never be interested in using football to engage and extend his son's education at nursery.

A truly inclusive environment will also take account of the needs of parents of children with disabilities. In theory they should be able to access the information and universal services anywhere; however, the reality is that they are not always thought about and, sadly, many are left unsupported for quite a long time before they get access to services such as childcare, carer support, home help, portage, and other specialist health practitioners such as occupational health. Too many systems of support are dependent on the child going through the statutory statementing process, which is often done as the child hits school age. Many children with less severe learning needs do not access support and help early so parents are left to cope with sometimes quite depressing results. The changes to the SEND may improve the situation but we will need to see how it is used especially when operating within shrinking local authority budgets.

Throughout this book, I have emphasised the role of leader as being someone who does not just make changes in their own setting but across the sector and beyond. In my view, the early years leader is at the heart of the Government's policy drive towards integrated seamless services across the sector, which I hope will result in multi-generational centres across the UK. Places where parents are not just seen as people with children under five but as people who are members of bigger families, living in local neighbourhoods and central players in making a difference to their own lives, their children's lives and the community in which they are trying to find a place and break the continuing cycle of social exclusion highlighted in the report from the End of Poverty Campaign (2008):

> Poverty affects children's health even before they are born, and the compounded consequences of poverty influence development throughout the lives of those who grew up poor. When they go on to have children of their own, these effects are passed to the next generation.
>
> (End of Poverty Campaign, 2008, p. 1)

If those of us leading children's services and organisations can help this process, we must know enough about the shape, dynamics and contribution of families to social cohesion to help them make it happen. For many of us this is a new journey. We have always worked with families because children are part of families, but now the expectation is deeper and we are expected to create services that support many families to move out of poverty, increase their parenting skills and confidence and contribute to creating a safer and happier communities. We, therefore, have a key role in informing the public debate about families, reminding politicians about the issues and keeping the needs of children and their families firmly on the political radar.

There are many complex factors which affect parenting but poverty is a significant one and it remains stubbornly high. Leaders in the early years need to understand this. Children and families living in poverty are still over-represented in statutory children's services and the children are still more likely to experience a range of barriers to success. The circumstances of a child's birth continue to play a substantial and increasing role in determining children's life chances; poorer children have a greater chance of failing than richer children.

Think and reflect!
Positive parenting

How do you measure up against the messages below?

Do you:

- Provide easily accessible information about positive parenting methods and parenting support services?
- Encourage staff to support parents to involve themselves in their children's play, learning and development?
- Encourage parents to be involved in the life of the service and give them the opportunity to influence planning and development?
- Have well-defined parent representation and communication channels so that feedback can be given easily?
- Regularly consult parents about their needs and actively seek to engage parents and help them understand what they can do to support their child's learning?
- Seek to create conditions in which parents feel confident about engaging in their child's learning and development and to seek help if they need?

Ideas for involving parents in activities

Here are some ideas to involve parents in early years settings. They have been given to me by other practitioners, with their comments, for which I am very grateful. Consider if they might work for you.

- Check your admission forms to ensure you get all the right information about dads.
    - *Dads loved our football topic and we ended up with a football match in the park. We had never met some of the dads before so it was great.*

- *We had a 'dads only' outing and we went to the art gallery with them. It was fun. They were much more relaxed about climbing, jumping and running so the children had lots of freedom.*
- *We did a science model gallery and dads had to help the children make a model over the weekend. It was great and they all took it very seriously.*

- Check what the parents in your setting would enjoy. For instance, consider holding a 'parents' week' with specific activities to encourage mums, dads and parents together.
  - *Our mums like coffee mornings if they are at home. So it is worth it for those Mums. Never seen a Dad at a coffee morning except to drop his wife off and collect her!*
  - *Evening workshops on the curriculum are a mainstay and get a good turn out of mums and dads. It's easier to come to them alone because they are planned to be interactive and 'have a go'.*
  - *Workshops for making props from household goods are popular with mums and dads. Props to use to sing songs at home, poetry pockets, nursery rhymes and storybooks. Very popular especially when run at 5 o'clock, so it is tagged on to collecting time.*
  - *Weekend books are resoundingly popular and the display that goes with them. Particularly popular with parents who are separated and see the children at the weekend. They then feature as part of the child's early learning life also.*
  - *A DVD of a selection of the week's activity on a loop in the hall is very popular.*
  - *Jazz Café, Arabic Dancing, International Fun Music Evening, all ideas which parents and staff enjoyed and participated in fully.*
  - *A DVD of a selection of the week's activity on a loop in the hall is very popular.*

- Think about going out . . .
  - *Trips near and far, because even when the trips are just local it certainly builds a social bond as you get to know another side of parents.*
  - *Healthy walks and then back to nursery to make soup with the chef.*
  - *We celebrated the end of the week with – a trip to the seaside.*

- . . .Or staying in!
  - *Lunches with parents and their children's key person works well, although a bit of a squash as all the parents come.*
  - *A DVD of a selection of the week's activity on a loop in the hall is very popular.*
  - *Lots of 'thank yous' displayed for the parents to see.*
  - *We provided cookbooks so parents could link eating at nursery to eating at home, especially for parents with children described as 'fussy eaters'.*

- Consider other family members as well.
  - *Celebrate grandparents with a 'bring your grandparents to nursery' event.*

Activities to complete at a staff team meeting or training session

These activities are provided to be used at a staff team meeting or training session to provoke discussion and to get the staff to think about how they would respond and what skills, knowledge and understanding they would use and why.

Activity 1

Here are some key questions for a staff meeting to check understanding about parental involvement.

1 Do all staff members actually know and understand the real impact of parental involvement on children's learning?

2 What do they understand by the concept of the Home Learning Environment ?

3 Do the staff use parents' knowledge of their children to influence how children can make progress?

4 Do staff use parents' insights into their children's learning to inform curriculum planning? If so, how?

5 Do staff know if parents' awareness of their potential impact on children's learning has changed, or can this change, the way they play with their children at home?

6 Are managers encouraging each staff member to develop a respectful and informed relationship with parents and share information?

Activity 2

Consider the following scenario:

You want to involve parents in your setting by giving them an independent voice and are looking at the best way to do it. You have three interconnected services and different sets of parents come to different services. You cannot manage three separate fora. You are quite anxious. You know all the positive reasons for involving parents, including children achieving more when their parents are involved, but in your previous setting the parents' group turned into a moaning group and also became quite a clique and you and your staff found the whole experience depressing and hard to manage. You have investigated the guidance from the government on setting up a parent council and discussed it with colleagues. Clearly the best parent group is one which understands its role as advisory and consultative with an important role in informing decision-making processes but not actually making decisions on behalf of the setting or getting involved in the daily running of the setting.

- How will you go about setting up a parents group so that you have a constructive relationship?
- How will you find the best ways of consulting all parents so as to get their input on decisions and development?

7 Developing new leaders

There is now a common expectation for leaders to create other leaders across the organisation. In 2003, the then Chief Inspector for Schools, David Bell, put forward the case for distributive leadership which he described as the means of developing leadership throughout a school so that the organisation is strengthened at every level and more able to meet new challenges. Others considered this concept of distributed leadership as a form of succession planning, especially as a leader of a growing organisation has less time to talk directly to the staff who are actually running the service and needs to find ways to ensure the organisational values, strategies and practice are operating correctly and consistently at every level of the organisation. The only way to do this is through a chain of command and therefore the need for real leadership lies further down that chain. I believe you need a team of leaders across the organisation who will spread the right message and gain the respect of their colleagues so the message is consistently implemented. As Whitaker (1993) said:

> Leadership is concerned with creating the conditions in which all members of the organisation can give of their best in a climate of commitment and challenge. Leadership helps an organisation to work well.
>
> (Whitaker, 1993, p. 74)

Kouzes and Posner (1999, p. 149) argued that the feature that separated effective from ineffective leaders was the degree to which they cared about the people they led. The Global Leadership Forecast (2007), a report which looked at leaders' shortcomings, showed that UK businesses were failing to improve leadership sufficiently in order to grow and compete. However, in terms of positive results, the majority of UK managers (67%) agreed that there was a strong emphasis on the alignment of leadership development with business priorities as well as performance management. The main reason given for poor development was companies failing to hold senior managers accountable.

Staff retention

Developing leadership across the organisation is considered by many to be a very good way of retaining staff and developing them so they help to grow and improve the organisation. Retaining of staff in the early years is a very significant issue and ways of encouraging successful retention will always be beneficial. The Effective Preschool Primary Education (EPPE) Report (2004) noted that low staff turnover was a key indicator in good-quality settings. There is much to be said for retaining good staff to give children and parents a feeling of stability. The average staff turnover in early years hovers at around 20% per annum, and that is a significant amount of staff to lose. There are many reasons for this level of turnover, not least the number of young staff, maternity leave, poor salaries and the sheer demands placed on staff in a fast-changing and highly demanding sector. It is worth noting that within the 18%, some experienced staff and potential leaders are lost. When staff leave they also take their experience and knowledge with them and that is much harder to replace. Of course, the reality is that not everyone will stay, not least because they may not be able to access the challenges and promotion they want and have to go elsewhere to get them. I always get a boost when a member of staff I have helped develop gets promoted across the sector. This is especially the case, as I believe that leaders have a duty to replenish and grow new leaders, not just within the organisation but also across the sector.

Understanding why people leave is critical both from a general perspective but also from a more in-depth and detailed basis in your own organisation. This understanding has to include the details of who is leaving and whether they are the leaders or staff with leadership ambition. Generally it appears that established leaders leave their organisations for three main reasons: first, they are on a career path and want to progress and this cannot be achieved if they stay where they are; second, they make a lifestyle change and leave at a point when they feel they have made a positive and significant contribution; and third, they go because they are burned out. This includes being overwhelmed by external inspection and regulation demands, dealing with increased aggression, unrelenting negative stress and insufficient praise, value and support.

There is much evidence that having a diverse workforce, and one which reflects the community in which you work and with whom you work, brings many advantages. In some instances having an approach which encourages development in the organisation actually enhances the diversity of the workforce, as it means people who are usually less likely to be given a chance are given a chance with you. Putting diversity at the heart of your organisation can open up new talent streams, broaden your approach and enhance the experience and understanding of how the organisation can better support families and communities. It can also create new business opportunities.

Back in 2008, the National College for School Leadership predicted a shortage of school leaders and stressed the need to develop more leaders, where possible using the wisdom of experienced leaders who tend to be strong in areas such as long-term thinking, political astuteness and indirect influencing. They suggested a balance of older and younger leaders, thereby requiring organisations to be constantly thinking about growing new leaders and retaining older ones so there is a continual transfer of ideas, skills and understanding by which the whole team is enhanced. Since the replacement of the NCSL with the National College of Teaching and Leadership in 2013, the emphasis on retaining staff remains.

The means of supporting the retention of staff, developing recruitment and replenishing the team is often referred to as 'succession planning'. Larger organisations see it as a sensible way of developing a competitive advantage because they are able to identify and replicate staff expertise and ensure there is never a point when the organisation is without the right balance of skills and expertise. It makes sense; but it is not always easy, especially in early years, where it is difficult to recruit high-calibre staff and growing your own takes time. Recruitment is a very expensive procedure and can cost up to 30% of an employee's annual salary, especially when you add in the costs of interviewing and all the administration that goes with it. This is not the sort of money that can easily be raised through initiatives, fundraising or grants and so has to come out of your hard-pressed core costs. It needs to be wisely invested. There is nothing more frustrating than either attracting a cohort of poor-quality staff, or no staff at all, having paid for an expensive advert and put a lot of effort into other forms of advertising. Succession planning is more likely to succeed if it is considered to be a part of the senior staff role and built into the organisational staff competences. Delegation is a key step towards bringing on a potential successor, but done in a way that is supportive. If there is a culture in the organisation to grow and support the development of all staff, then it is more likely to happen consistently.

Succession planning is, therefore, a sensible solution. Growing and nurturing your own talented staff, developing their capabilities to retain their expertise and knowledge of the organisation and your place in the sector gives a message to other staff that you value them and are willing to invest in them for the long term. A setting's reputation for career development can also improve recruitment and retention, with talented potential recruits persuaded to join because of an employer's commitment to career progression.

Finally, on a more pragmatic level, if, as a leader, you have sweated blood and tears to get the quality of service to the children and families up to a good standard, you do not want to see your good work undone, or your shoes filled, by an ineffectual leader who can talk the talk at interview but cannot commit to the complexities of leading an excellent service.

> If you want to build a ship, don't drum up the people to gather wood, divide the work and give orders, teach them to yearn for the vast and endless sea.
>
> (Saint Exupéry, www.brainyquotes.com/quotes)

If you want to retain staff at their best and for the length of time best suited for you and them, I believe you need to do two things. First, articulate your understanding of leadership in your setting so they know what to expect. Second, create a learning organisation which is built on the principles of what makes people happy at work so they want to give their best and stay with you.

When Charlie Banks, the boss of Wolseley, the biggest distributor of heating and plumbing products, was asked what leadership meant to him, he replied:

> It's about being able to put together your ideas; convince people that it's the right thing to do; and to provide direction and example that makes them want to execute it. I feel that you get a

lot better support if people understand what it is you are trying to do. They see you putting as
much energy and passion in it as you want them to – or more. Then they'll go along.

(Edge, 2004 p. 17)

How to develop leaders

To lead you need to be able to articulate what you understand by leadership. It is not going to happen by having a tick list that you share with staff but, given the complexities of characteristics, competencies and leadership traits (see Chapter 2), it is very important that staff understand what you mean by leadership. We have ascertained that context is critical in leadership and as the early years sector is very diverse and fast-changing, so we need to communicate our personal understanding of good leadership within our own setting.

If there is one lesson that should have come out of all the recent research into leadership, it's that
the situation is the most important factor. There are at least two major elements to this – how do
you become a leader in the first place and what do you do when you get there?

(Edge, 2005 p. 9)

Leadership or, most importantly, effective leadership seems to have some common themes across all sectors. A frequent one is the ability to set out a vision, communicate it clearly at every level and get staff to buy into it, understand what is expected of them and how to make it real. In early years, the vision will usually include the ability to create a high-quality learning environment for children, staff and families.

Leaders need to shape staff to learn to become resilient and be able to manage the demands of leadership. It is essential for their success in what will be a challenging, complex and worthwhile role. Good leaders have the ability to be self-aware and can read and manage situations which cause pain and difficulty. They also have developed systems to support themselves, whether through mentoring, having external interests or just knowing where to go to unload safely.

Learning about target setting

Successful leaders tend not to be perfectionists and head for the 80%, which can be achieved in small steps. They will not burn themselves out trying to get perfection every time; sometimes pragmatism is all about deciding whether it is worth killing yourself for the last 20% when the return is minimal. To help staff develop it is important to help them understand whether they have achieved their intended goal, so setting clear targets in the first place with a real example of what that looks like in reality is the key. People often call them 'performance measurements', 'key performance indicators' or 'measurement outcomes'. but I think that this sort of language can be a bit unnerving, especially for younger staff and then, immediately, negative stress starts to build. Instead, think encourage them to consider what their goal will look like when it is achieved; eventually it will become less daunting for them to read the target and understand its meaning. Targets are best managed when they are understood and made meaningful. That way it is possible to challenge the reality of the target. For example: is it possible to convert a target for increased occupancy by 15% in a difficult market? Why 15%? Is this an arbitrary figure set by someone who doesn't understand or is it critical to sustainability? Can you reduce realistically the number of parents' com- plaints by 2% or measure food waste by the plateful?

Targets are set to help gain a focus on getting an improvement. They are of little use if they are neither understood nor accepted. To help leaders develop, encourage them to take control of target setting and make it work for them.

The concept of quality

Leaders need to be very informed and knowledgeable about how children and adults learn and what is needed to facilitate this. Leaders need to be able to recognise good care and education and have a whole set of systems and structures to ensure that this is achieved at every level. It is necessary to keep in mind that the concept of quality is itself highly problematic. The language of quality is often used to give credit to the maze of regulations in early years, which can actually undermine rather than support professional independence. Leaders needs to clarify the concept of quality to all the other leaders developing under their guidance. This means being able to articulate what quality looks like in the setting at every level of practice and then being able to apply it. Leaders need to be able to explain how and what research has been the basis for the rationale employed, given the importance research has in bridging the gap between policy and practice. However, it is necessary to guard against the risk that, although we may believe that our action research is objective, our perceptions (like it or not!) of what constitutes quality are deeply and quietly influenced by societal context and the ensuing regulations and policy frameworks. Leaders must build a team culture and encourage research and reflection at every level but in a way that enhances meaning and allows for full and frank debate and dialogue, particularly as working with children presents many questions, and the answers are not always either neat or logical.

Forming relationships

Early years leaders need to apply emotional intelligence when forming and maintaining relationships and when encouraging relationship building across the organisation, with other networks and out in the community. It is through relationships that people develop an attachment and loyalty to the organisation and ultimately to the sector, with the overarching ambition of making a difference in the long term. Therefore, good leaders show they care about the people they lead and are secure enough to distribute this leadership so that eventually they can leave an organisation secure and robust. In some ways, when articulating a view of leadership leaders need to be writing themselves out of a job in the long term.

> *Leaders are able to balance the concern for work, task, quality and productivity with concern for people, relationships, satisfaction and morale. They combine an orientation towards innovation and change with an interest in continuity and stability for the present. They do this by using personal qualities which command respect and promote feelings of trust and security. They are also responsible for setting and clarifying goals, roles and responsibilities, collecting information and planning, making decisions and involving members of the group by communicating, encouraging and acknowledging commitment and contribution.*
>
> (Rodd, 1998, p.2)

Leadership versus management

One area that needs exploring when thinking about views on leadership is the clash between the concepts of leadership and management. If you want to create new leaders then it is wise to at least consider the possibilities of there being a difference between managers and leaders. Growing managers is an important task, but if there are other factors that make a manager a leader, and if it is the leadership element that makes the more significant difference to the service, then it is critical that this is recognised at the earliest stage.

> *We will only be successful if our services have the right quality of leadership and management. We need leaders and managers who can build teams competent and confident in this new means of service delivery; who will put the child and family first; who can lead those from outside their own areas of expertise; who can manage resources in new ways; and who can reconcile team members' different working practices and expectations.*
>
> (Championing Children 2006, p. 2)

Larkin (2008) described the experience of people working for leaders and managers as different. According to him, those who work for someone who is namely a manager are usually unhappy at work. He says they:

- Work to the minimum standards
- Only do what is required
- Fear change in case it means extra work
- Operate in an environment based on fear and suspicion
- Work together as a team to survive their manager

- Are punished for mistakes and strive not to be caught next time

- Look forward to going home

- Are aiming for a future elsewhere.

(Larkin, 2008, p. 19)

Whereas those who work for a leader:

- Are more productive

- Produce higher-quality work

- Are more motivated

- Go that extra mile

- Embrace change and take on new challenges readily

- Operate in an environment based on trust and mutual respect

- Work together as a team to support their leader

- Learn from their mistakes and strive for better next time

- Look forward to coming to work

- Are aiming for future goals.

(Larkin, 2008, p. 19)

An interesting summary is made by Gold and Evans (1998) who suggested that 'within these definitions, it seems that management and leadership overlap . . . but leadership has an almost spiritual dimension, paying more attention to beliefs and values' (p. 26).

It would seem that leaders give more direction to staff and identify goals and ambitions for the organisation with relevant structures to support them. Managers are expected to convert these goals and ambitions into policies and action plans and implement them, analysing and problem-solving as they go along. Leaders are meant to inspire and motivate and come up with ideas, while the manager makes them happen but also inspires and encourages staff to turn the big plan into reality. Leaders build their teams to work with them to take the organisation forward and do so through consultation and collaboration. The manager has to manage the performance of the team and ensure the actual work is done satisfactorily and that staff are getting the right support, training, praise and encouragement to keep the show on the road. Clearly there is some overlapping in the roles and tasks of leaders and managers but there are also some distinct differences in how to achieve the same goal; an organisation which does what it says on the tin. I like Hall's (1996) very thoughtful idea that leadership is actually philosophy in action. She did not discount management, in fact she sees it as integral, and then summed up her point by stating that to lead without managing is irresponsible, but to manage without leading is unethical. The leadership–management debate is an interesting one and is a catalyst to provoke some philosophical discussion with staff. For me, emotional intelligence is a significant factor in successful leadership and is common in those leaders considered to be outstanding performers. In reality, this is transformed into the leader's ability to set a good example, apply the values of the organisation at every level and be sensitive and empathetic to staff and respond thoughtfully with understanding and integrity. Leaders need:

> ... to focus on the inner experiences, values and understanding of the professional involved. Leadership work is inordinately unpredictable, depending upon variables which cannot always be identified. The processes involved in helping leaders to develop effectiveness require reflection, intellectual grappling and intuitive sharpness, rather than learning prescribed strategies and tactics ... Leadership and management are not so much about structures, systems and procedures, as about principles, values and understanding.
>
> ('Introduction' to *Pen Green National Professional Qualification in Integrated Leadership*, 2004)

Supporting staff as they develop into new leaders

At LEYF we prepare staff for the leadership role through our Challenge Support and Inspire programme, which focuses on each person looking into their hearts and considering what kind of a leader they will be and whether, through that, they can lead others. We also have the Aspiring Leaders programme for those aspiring to take leadership roles in the organisation. The programme focuses on a balance of leadership skills, business management and personal emotional intelligence to help get staff to understand the complexities of the leadership roles.

To develop new leaders, it is important to support them in a variety of ways. It is necessary to understand what they want and how we keep them motivated and satisfied at work. This means giving consideration to the work environment, the balance and quality of work, motivational factors, the work–life balance, independence, initiative and progression. Also, it is thought that a value-led organisation that has the intention of trying to help others tend to have higher retention rates. According to Ben Cohen and Jerry Greenfield, co-founders of Ben & Jerry's ice cream:

> When you're value led, you're trying to help the community. And when you're trying to help the community, people want to buy from you. They want to work for you. They want to be associated with you. They feel invested in your success.
>
> (Cohen and Greenfield, 1997, p.29)

The chance to make a difference in the company of talented colleagues is perhaps the ultimate retention tool. Raising self-esteem and morale through directly involving staff in the leadership and management of their setting has many positive outcomes. According to research from

Roffey Park, the key to making sure that knowledge is kept within the organisation is to give staff the chance to tackle some interesting and innovative projects. However, Maslow (1943) took us right back to basics, stating that staff needed their basic needs fulfilled before they could aim for their own personal achievement, both intrinsically through job satisfaction and extrinsically through good work conditions. In a modern economy, people can achieve basic needs more easily and quickly and work instead for satisfaction, impact, achievement and growth. Herzberg et al. (1959) looked at the factors which negatively affected motivation leading to dissatisfaction. In current early years these factors may include:

- Poor levels of pay
- Too much external change
- Too much paperwork
- Too many inspections and competing monitoring regimes
- Inadequate building, particularly when hiring temporary space and having to get everything out and put it away everyday
- Inadequate outdoor space, stuck in the middle of a concrete jungle
- A team with high levels of sickness and discontent.

Some of these things can be improved and reduced; others cannot be addressed easily, but if you can get the balance right the frustration will settle down and staff will be able to enjoy the actual work, in this case working with children and families. It also allows staff to gain a sense of recognition and enough authority and responsibility to make decisions or take risks and achieve something, as well as opportunities to master a new skill and coaching and mentoring opportunities. To support staff to become new leaders, it is important to enable them to move to a place where they believe their voice is heard as well as having the chance to be involved. It is also important to explore with them opportunities for promotion, progression, sabbaticals and personal recognition and reward.

It is always worth evaluating and re-evaluating staff benefits and considering what is possible in terms of salary, flexible working, better holidays, long- service rewards, childcare support, salary sacrifice, pensions and any other fringe benefits such as lunch or vouchers. The best way of motivating staff is to give them what they really want most from work. The more you can provide of what they want, the more you can expect from them in return: namely, an effective quality service where you make a difference to everyone who comes through the door. Getting the staff to feel they really make a difference and will leave a mark on the community is critical; achievement and celebration is at the heart of this.

Moving out of the 'comfort zone'

The Vygotsky principle of the zone of further development is one that can be used to help staff move out of their comfort zone by offering new and interesting opportunities.

It will only work if those staff are provided with the necessary support to meet the new demands made of them. It seems obvious but, despite all the information around, it i's not unusual for someone to be given a new personal challenge and then left to get on with it. It resonates with the old-fashioned way of teaching someone to swim by throwing them in at the deep end on the basis they will either sink or swim. I sank and cannot swim to this day! If you genuinely want staff to succeed with a new challenge, then plan it and give them preparation, access to the right support (this may be no more than a book and a policy) and the power to lead an idea, a project or a team. How many times are staff encouraged to lead a new project and not given a small budget or the right authority to actually do the job? It is not much good if they have to come back to you at every stage to get funds and permissions. Give them the right support by letting them have the space to do the job.

The right support is a fine line. Too much interference and you undermine the staff member; leaving them to flounder is also unlikely to result in success. Some people see delegation as a form of development but others turn delegation into dumping on staff. Leaders of effective settings know the difference between delegating and dumping. There is also a skill in helping people to recognise that they are ready to lead. Giving them the opportunity too soon may result in too many mistakes, causing anxiety and a loss of confidence for staff members as well as from their colleagues. Getting the moment right is important, so think carefully about who to develop and then plan how to help them move towards leadership. Make sure to consider the impact on any other staff and how they might feel.. Not everyone takes kindly to a colleague getting new opportunities, no matter how just and fair it is. In fact, I have been surprised by the reaction of some staff to my encouraging another's initiative and ability. It was perceived as favouritism. Supporting staff, no matter how rational and correct the reason can elicit a jealous reaction from other staff and often from those who show neither initiative nor interest. It can shock you; so be prepared and try and be as fair and transparent as possible.

Create an ethos where staff are encouraged to take risks. Of course, this still means thinking something through and having a rationale for action. If it then goes awry or the outcome is spoiled by unexpected and unforeseen circumstances leading to a mistake, then see the learning potential of the mistake. Design a response procedure so the mistake becomes learning for everyone across the organisation. Don't go in for the blame game; it just causes unhappiness, fear and an unwillingness to try anything new in the future. It also de-motivates staff who become worried and anxious.

According to Bennett et al. (2003), an effective setting has a team of staff who share a common understanding of the organisation and possess a common understanding of its aims and ways of working. A learning organisation will embed this even more powerfully through a common commitment to learning together through action research, reflection, critical quest and professional development.

Know your staff

One way of ensuring that leadership is delegated and supported across the organisation efficiently is to know your staff. There are many types of team members and sometimes it is easy to put them 'in a box'. It took me ten years to get an anxious member of staff to become a deputy. I knew she had it in her; she achieved all the small steps and surprised herself when she saw her name on the website with the title 'deputy manager' written against it.

Even though leaders should be keen and optimistic to support staff development, it makes sense also to listen to colleagues. They often see a different side to someone. I remember inheriting a very obstreperous staff member. I could not see how she could be developed; but her manager saw way beyond my narrow view and knew that someone who worked so well with children had something positive buried inside. She released the potential through nurturing and coaching and she is now a superb early years professional. I have made lots of mistakes in my time by choosing people I found to be naturally charismatic and giving them lots of opportunities. However, once they achieved their goals, they became arrogant and, in my view, spoiled all their successes by failing to be respectful and empathetic to their colleagues. I guess that we have all been taken in by the charmer who seemed like a person with huge possibilities but then, put under the spotlight, like Icarus, they melted.

As well as choosing the right staff and giving them the right challenge it is important to consider different learning styles. The principle of lifelong learning and, in particular, David Kolb's (1984) idea that you can continue to acquire new knowledge by having the idea and the theory and making sense of them through real experiences is fantastic. This way, learners continually strive for an ever-greater balance between themselves and an increasingly complex environment. In searching for the answers they open up new ways of thinking, more learning experiences and greater degrees of initiative and responsibility.

Staff thrive if they are helped to learn in the way they feel most comfortable. I particularly like providing opportunities that staff can use quite quickly in the workplace; for example, training someone to use software to present their idea or research findings to the staff and then later to parents.

Action learning

Some settings use action learning to support staff. It has been described as the best way to bring life experience to the fore and the single most important resource in enabling the individual to move forward in their learning and development with the support of others.

Action learning is based on someone asking questions about an aspect of their work as it relates to the organisational objectives. An example could be a colleague sharing a concern such as describing a member of staff who appears to dislike another and seems to act in a bullying manner; the children appear to notice and parents have alluded to this behaviour happening outside also. This could then be critically analysed by the group in such a way that they learn more about their part in leading, responding to and managing the situation and then resolving it in a way that moves them forward. It is another type of learning that encourages self-reflection and better self-awareness, all of which supports better leadership.

> Today's ever changing business environment demands that managers are well- rounded, multi-talented people able to handle a wide variety of roles. With this in mind, individuals are increasingly taking responsibility for their own development.
>
> (Ashridge, 2005)

Everyone wants to work for an organisation that is successful and which has a good reputation. As a leader, this sets you a target to create an environment in which the setting is guaranteed a reputation for quality and high standards in the community and sector as far as is possible. I believe that having action research as a core principle of practice and a core strand of a learning organisation helps ensure quality. Action research, or, simply put, asking critical questions and reflecting about what might be done in particular situations in order to create a better understanding and improve actual practice, is essential for staff development. It also means leadership principles are established at every level of the organisation, beginning with the children.

Developing yourself

Leaders need to be more knowledgeable than their staff and take their own learning seriously so as to provide intellectual stimulation for their staff along with ongoing support. This needs to be done on two levels, through personal relationships and through the systems in place.

Many settings have an appraisal system; others have personal development plans. Some settings have a coaching programme from induction, which is a great way to help people learn on the job, especially when discovering how 'we do things around here'. It can also be a good development opportunity for the coach as well and can bring the best out in people. It certainly helps connect the 'doing' with the 'why': something that is not always clear to staff. Having a mentor is another useful tool for self-development. It can help you develop self-awareness which helps personal and professional integration. It is also a place where you can safely address conflict in your own head when trying to address complex issues and work out personal motivations which can become blurred. Good mentors offer constructive feedback which can lead to personal self-assessment and greater self-awareness. As emotional intelligence is vital to effective leadership, opportunities to learn more about yourself can only enrich your leadership.

Recently, more organisations have started introducing sabbaticals, once the realm of universities. These career breaks are unpaid and usually considered for staff who have been with the organisation for a long time, as an employee benefit. Other opportunities can include time to attend conferences, to visit other settings near and far, job swaps, participating in and leading policy workshops, representing the sector on committees, learning networks, leading a research project, membership of relevant associations and institutes, and access to advanced training and qualification programmes.

Being part of a learning organisation

A true learning organisation is always ready to listen to a request as well as keep an eye out for new experiences for staff. An interesting way of sharing your leadership is by preparing others to become a trustee and ultimately the chair of a trustee board. In that way they are not only developing their personal leadership skills and applying them in a new context, they are also contributing to growing and sustaining another organisation. Many people are frightened of becoming trustees because they believe they do not know enough or do not have the right skills and experience or because they feel that it is too great a responsibility. However, once a trustee has the right insurance and works with the best of intentions to do the right thing for the organisation, then the risk of ending up accused of failing to exercise due diligence and a duty of care is much reduced.

The first test of a leader is that he leaves behind him in other men the conviction and the will to carry on.

(Walter Lippman, quoted in Ratcliffe, 2000, p. 218)

It is not always easy to nurture leaders, particularly in a sector with a high turnover and where many of the staff do not think they have a very high value. Therefore, leaders in early years need to contribute to the debate on professionalism and what constitutes the early years professional. Leaders must raise the profile of early years leaders at every level of an organisation and put leadership and learning at the heart of an organisation.

Leaders who take a stand and think bravely about what future early years leaders need to look like, how they should behave and what they need to achieve will reap rewards in terms of staff loyalty, higher retention and a better service. Creating a supportive organisation which has a learning ethos running through its very core is the best way to ensure that staff gain a sense of self-worth because they recognise that the organisation wants to invest in them and build on their knowledge, skills and understanding.

If organisations want to grow leaders – or at least create the conditions necessary for growth – they can do no better than to give potential leaders the chance to lead.

(Adair, 2005, p. 11)

Top tips

To encourage new leaders give them plenty of appropriate:

- Opportunities to take responsibility and initiative
- Opportunities to make decisions
- Opportunities to communicate using a range of media
- Coaching to help prepare them to deal with inevitable setbacks and impediments to success.

Think and reflect!

Checklist for developing new leaders

Given the importance of growing and retaining leaders in your setting, use the questions below to check whether you are developing new leaders in your setting and if they are positioned in the right place and likely to stay.

- Do you know who your most effective leaders are?
- Are they getting the right experiences?
- Are they positioned in the right places?
- How are you benefiting from their leadership skills?
- What would the consequences be if they left?
- Do you know why people leave your setting?
- Of those who have left, how many were leaders or potential leaders?
- Are there improvements that could be made that would reduce these losses?
- Have you a succession plan?

Identifying a starting point for the new leader

The following are a set of statements to use with someone who has become a new leader. They can be used as confirmation of knowledge, points of discussion or as the basis of a personal development plan.

- What are the values of your organisation?
- What do they look like in practice?
- Do you know what the organisation's strategic vision is? If not, do you know where to find it?

- Could you describe this to your colleagues in a way they understand?
- Who are the service users and stakeholders of your organisation? Do you know the difference?
- Can you name any of them?
- Who is the chair of governors or board of trustees?
- What is your idea of quality in the setting?
- Can you describe how your setting supports equality and inclusivity?
- Can you describe how the EYFS rolls out in your setting?
- Do you know about compliance and which laws regulate your service?
- Do know where to go for help when required?
- If you had a magic wand, what three things would you change?
- If you had a magic wand, what three things would you like to help you make these changes?

8 The entrepreneurial leader: leading a childcare social enterprise

The late Peter Drucker predicted that the twenty-first century would be a time when the social organisation would come to the fore. The more the economy, money and information became global, the more community would matter. He believed that the charitable, voluntary and social enterprise sectors, often referred to collectively as the third sector, would most likely take advantage of emerging opportunities and mobilise local resources to solve community problems. The leadership of this sector would therefore be influential in determining the values, vision, cohesion and performance of modern life.

> *The most effective global citizens will be those that succeed emerging their business and philanthropic missions to build a future of shared prosperity and shared responsibility.*
> (President Bill Clinton, *The Financial Times*, 2012)

The ethos of many early years settings sits quite comfortably with Drucker's vision. Perhaps our time has come? Many settings, particularly in the third sector, were set up to help create communities where sharing and support is fostered in order to lead to better health, lower crime, improved educational performance and greater life satisfaction. The fact that the government is now following this lead with policy initiatives presents another set of opportunities.

Social enterprises have received much approval of late and are an increasingly popular part of our national economy. A social enterprise is a business that trades in the market with a social purpose. It is not defined by its legal status but by its nature, aims and outcomes. The profits of a social enterprise are principally reinvested in the business to achieve social objectives. Social enterprises can come in many forms including cooperatives, credit unions, community businesses, development trusts and housing associations. Charities can also operate as social enterprises and many community nurseries are social enterprises in ethos and business models

> *Social enterprise is about people. Social entrepreneurs run profitable businesses that reject exploitation and instead choose to invest in society's most disadvantaged people.*
> (Ogden-Newton, 2007 p. 2)

Social enterprise also captures the sense of a movement led by people who want to challenge the status quo and create a shift in attitude. Social enterprises are willing to tackle some of the most entrenched social and environmental challenges in an innovative way.

> *The social enterprises and social entrepreneurship movement is driving a big change. It is influencing the private sector to take ethical values into account, the public sector to be more focused on users in its delivery of public services, and charities to develop trading activities.*
>
> (Robb, 2007, p. 4)

Many leaders in early years are not aware of the impact they have on society. Often they are humble and modest and would never think they could offer good advice to wider government and society. Yet leaders of all social enterprises can challenge and help governments to improve the way public services are designed, commissioned and delivered. They can help explore the concept of the social return on investment and measure the value-added contribution of their services. Leaders must share innovative ideas and have a 'can-do' attitude, especially if they are to help build community cohesion and reach what governments like to refer to as the 'hard to reach' communities. No community is that hard to reach: it is the services that are hard to reach. The following quote helps, I think, to put this in perspective.

> *Many participants welcome the chance to take responsibility and to learn and work with other people from other walks of life. People are always more secure knowing first hand where others stand and may begin in this setting to accept differences – in background, viewpoints and values – as realities to be lived with, not problems to be solved.*
>
> (Weisbord and Janoff, 2000, p. 10)

There is no doubt that finding pioneering ways of challenging inherent social problems is important, but ultimately the entrepreneurial leader must combine social and environmental responsibility with financial success and balance the books. In other words, making money in a way that fits with personal and organisational values.

Many people in the early years sector see making money as the root of all evil, but, without money, new opportunities cannot be created.. If, however, making money and a profit is linked effectively to social purpose it can be the root of opportunity.

In her paper 'Social enterprise: the case for definition' (2007), Jennifer Bradley warned that social entrepreneurship is an appealing construct precisely because it holds such high promise. If that promise is not fulfilled because too many 'non- entrepreneurial' efforts are included in the definition, then social entrepreneurship will fall into disrepute, and the kernel of true social entrepreneurship will be lost.

This is particularly important if you are leading an organisation in the early years sector (irrespective of how you define yourself). Understanding entrepreneurial leadership will help those in charge to lead and develop the organisation, especially as many people think that socially enterprising leaders can make a difference to and influence others to create a fairer society. They are seen as taking on new battles, no matter how unpopular the idea, and finding solutions to difficult issues.

> *Social entrepreneurship signals the imperative to drive social change, and it is that potential payoff, with its lasting, transformational benefit to society, that sets the field and its practitioners apart.*
>
> (Bradley, 2007 p. 1)

Why convert the idea into a childcare setting?

Entrepreneurial leaders tend to start from a clear value base and build those values into the way they do business, not just superficially, such as giving a donation, but in exploring in-depth how the business operation can benefit society. This is quite important as, like it or not, business is one of the most powerful forces in society and, therefore, business has a responsibility for the welfare of society as a whole. This responsibility places an immediate requirement on the entrepreneurial leader to understand the importance of running a sustainable business and to do this in a way that adds value to the community and maximises its impact by integrating socially beneficial actions into as many of its day-to-day activities as possible. In order to do that, the values must be led from the top and must be integral to the organisation's vision, strategy and operating plan. A strategy is best summed up in three questions:

- Where are we now?
- Where are we going?
- How are we going to get there?

The way this noble ambition is converted into an organisational ethos and operational plan will depend on many factors, including governance, environment, opportunity, staffing, financial structure and community input. However, as we already know that what we do can make a difference, we need to focus on how well we do it so we can make a significant difference.

The concept of running a socially conscious organisation, in whatever shape, fits well with childcare. All societies should take special care of their youngest members. Sinclair (2006) referred to Grunewald, an economic analyst who argued that if the government invested substantially in parenting and enriched daycare now they could expect a rate of return of 3:1 to 7:1 and expect to achieve a return of 17:1 by the time the child reaches 21 years of age. The social benefits would also be significant and included a reduction in crime and prison occupancy, better educational attainment, healthier adults and reduced levels of obesity and reduction in welfare dependency. According to Alan Sinclair:

> *Early engagement pays a very high rate of return. The dividend is 12–16% per year for every £1 of investment – a payback of four or five times the original investment by the time the young person reaches their early twenties and the gains continue to flow throughout their life.*
>
> (Sinclair, 2006, p. 5)

Such considerations also fit with the growing wealth of compelling evidence from neuroscience to support the idea of a critical period of learning in the very earliest years. Of a child's achievement, 80% is dependent on their backgrounds. The variables that influence a child's success and life chances include:

- Family
- Social capital
- Social class
- Poverty
- Early years education and care
- Personality
- Motivation
- Ability.

Too many negative ticks in the box and a child is already facing disadvantage and, by the time a child has reached 22 months, the gap between poorer and richer children has begun to widen considerably. According to the Unicef report (2007), children in the UK had the poorest quality of life in the developed world with poor results for educational well-being, relationship formation, risk-taking behaviour and general happiness. As early years leaders we have little time to make a difference so what we do matters. Understanding the community within which the child lives is very important as the social context is significant in terms of how we create services and what they should look like. The term 'community' is used very casually but for many families there is no such thing as community. They live lonely, sad and frightened lives in neighbourhoods rife with:

- Drug dealing and usage
- High levels of family dysfunction
- High levels of mental health and instability
- Increasing crime or fear of crime
- Domestic violence
- Litter and fear in open and outside spaces
- Loneliness and social isolation among indigenous and immigrant families
- Poverty
- Stressful relationships
- Tolerance of higher levels of aggression.

Understanding what community means for those children likely to use the early years service is important. Sharing a neighbourhood does not equal community. If we are to help local people to create some form of community spirit and community cohesion, then we need to understand the complexities of building up relationships that will eventually lead to people wanting to be a part of the local community and part of a group that becomes affirming and deep-rooted. Metaphorically, this group will continue to ripple out from a centre, since individuals drop in a stone which is made from a shared and meaningful purpose. If this is the basis of our approach, then we need to create an organisation that weaves the means of developing community relationships and networks into its very structure. The starting point is how we address and enrich the real experiences of local children and their families, which may well include emotional poverty, insecure parenting, lack of self-belief and a dependence on celebrity culture, media myths and cheap TV?

The early years is also the time when children are actively learning to make sense of their world. They assimilate information from experiences in various contexts: their own immediate family, their wider community and society in general. Research suggests that the status of children's reference group will influence the level of resilience they will have in the face of possible future experiences of discrimination and prejudice. As children develop their awareness and understanding about community groups they are constructing 'theories' about diversity, congruent with their general cognitive stages of development as well as their life experiences. Adults' reactions to children's questions may fail to give them the help they need to form positive ideas about themselves or positive dispositions towards others who are different. This is very significant when trying to prepare children for their role in their neighbourhoods but also in creating future social entrepreneurs who can shape the communities they want for themselves. The role of the entrepreneurial leader is therefore very significant in terms of how the organisation contributes to community learning and involvement. It's not just about the immediate but very much about the future.

Entrepreneurial leaders are therefore looking at ways of creating social capital. Putnam (2000) said that social capital is second only to poverty in the breadth and depth of its affect on children's lives.

Child development is powerfully shaped by social capital ... trust, networks and norms of reciprocity within a child's family, school, peer groups and larger community have wide ranging effects on the child's opportunities and choices and hence behaviour and development.

(Putnam, 2000, p. 296)

Childcare organisations operating from a social values base can contribute to community cohesion and even fight poverty by creating employment and offering education and training to adults to make them economically independent. They can also offer children social capital which gives them the knowledge and confidence to better understand the world and help them access it with greater assurance. Making the service fully accessible to all, including real ways of engaging and involving people, consulting and responding to what they want and need and using entrepreneurial skills to create innovative, creative and inspirational responses, gives a clear message that getting it right matters.

Archbishop Desmond Tutu described social capital in terms of the South African concept of Ubantu:

We say a person is a person through persons. We don't come fully formed into the world. We learn how to think, how to walk, how to speak, how to behave, indeed how to be human, from other human beings. We need other human beings in order to be human. We are made for togetherness, we are made for a family, for fellowship. To exist in a tender network of interdependence…This is how you have Ubantu – you care, you are hospitable, you're gentle, you're compassionate and concerned.

(Battle, 1997, p. 65)

Principles for successful communities

When you think about how you can help community cohesion, consider the principles which make successful communities. It helps articulate what you want to create to make a positive change. These include:

- Agreed and explicit social norms and values

- High levels of trust, openness, consistency and reliability

- A clear understanding and ability to be good citizens

- A clear moral consensus as the basis of how local decisions are made

- Sophisticated social networks with lines of communication that have a shared language, common vocabulary and high-quality conversation

- Symbols and rituals that weave a tapestry of identity

- A culture of people looking out for each other

- An environment where people join in, volunteer, get involved or give something back.

The social entrepreneurial leader in action

The leadership responsibility has now broadened to include us acting as social entrepreneurs, so as to make a difference both immediately and in the long term to children and families in terms of their education and care but also to the community in which they live and grow. To do this leaders need to be transformative so that they can shape and raise the goals and motivations of others who need challenging. Shea summed this up when he advised that:

Modern leadership is more to do with inspiration or influence, manipulating people and getting them to follow you, making your goals and theirs the same. Good leadership is to do with personal bonding skills, bad leadership introduces the heavy hand of sanctions. Relationship between the leaders and the led should be a voluntary one.

(Shea, 1990, p. 21)

McCelland (1961) suggested that social entrepreneurs have an overwhelming need for achievement. They have a vision and are able to see and act on opportunities. They are calculated risk takers and innovative, with a high internal locus of control. They are assertive and have the ability to commit to others. John Spedan Lewis (1885–1963), one of our enduring social entrepreneurs, said that it is all wrong to have millionaires before you have ceased to have slums. His answer was the John Lewis Partnership, which he believed made work something to live for as well as something to make a difference.

Timmons (1994) considered entrepreneurship as a process, where the entrepreneur creates or seizes an opportunity and pursues it, regardless of whether the resources are available and they will use all their ingenuity to access any relevant resources possible. Kao (1986) referred to the work of Burch, who found that common traits in entrepreneurs included an ability to work hard, nurture quality, accept responsibility, remain optimistic and seek out reward, not just in terms of money but in recognition and respect. He described entrepreneurs as keen observers of human behaviour with an eclectic interest in information and a powerful imagination. He said that entrepreneurs show:

The capacity to work exceptionally hard in pursuit of a particular project [that] requires a combination of physical, emotional and intellectual energy which cannot be artificially stimulated except in short bursts . . . The extraordinary feat of the entrepreneur is to sustain their commitment and capacity in the long term.

(Kao, 1986, p. 11)

Entrepreneurs are perceived as having a heightened sense of curiosity which they use to spot a gap or make a link; then having observed the possibility, they act. This could be by demanding or making a new and better service or product, or developing a new venture from some change in the economic, legal or business climate. Their satisfaction comes from solving the problem rather than making money.

Social entrepreneurs worth their salt do not follow conventional ways of working. Their view of the world begins with people, passion, experience and story – not policy, statistics and theory.

(Mawson, 2008, p. 2)

Deakins (1996) developed the role of self in entrepreneurship when he introduced the entrepreneur as a continual learner. He suggested that:

Entrepreneurship involves a learning process, an ability to cope with problems and to learn from those problems. An ability to recognise why the problems occur and to be able to deal with them and more importantly understand why they occur will ensure that the entrepreneur will be able not only to deal with those problems but learn from the experience and ensure that processes are out in place within the firm to ensure that either the problem does not occur again or that the firm can deal with the problem.

(Deakins, 1996, p 21)

Entrepreneurial leaders are alert to the changing political, social, economic and technological contexts which affect organisational culture, expectations and workplace requirements and, in turn, generate new challenges to leadership. According to Leadbeater (1997) entrepreneurial organisations develop a culture of trust to encourage creativity because creativity comes when there is trust. This is also important in the way they help form an enterprising team. The leader does not necessarily complete the task alone. Sykes (1999) described three contributions which together could make a real difference. The envisioner spots the opportunity and possibly identifies an inventive way to respond; the enabler gets together the relevant people, funds and means of making it happen, and the enacter manages the project so it concludes successfully. This is often best seen when an idea is shaped by an enterprising leader and then colleagues from other local agencies and local people work together to make it happen.

Enterprising leaders create enterprising teams with 'go-getting' attitudes and a desire for consistently high standards. In fact, they have all the characteristics of a successful leader but with an enterprising twist. Being able to adapt and manage change through an ethos of problem-solving features high on the list, as does the need to remain grounded in realism. Maintaining a sense of humour is a quality that can never be underestimated; provided it is used appropriately, it is a marker of successful survival.

However, as Kao (1986) pointed out, entrepreneurship is increasingly synonymous with 'good', to the extent that entrepreneurs are viewed as new cultural heroes and therefore critical examination of their characteristics can be obscured by media hype or collective beliefs. As leaders, we have to be careful we don't lose touch with reality and begin believing the hype.

There is a benefit to being seen as a socially enterprising leader wanting to build and transform a community into one that cares for itself. Socially enterprising organisations also benefit in terms of positive staff relations. It appears that, in the minds of the employees of social enterprises, these aspects of the job outweigh many of the negatives and make them desirable places to work. This finding is reiterated by Aviva, the UK's largest insurance service provider: 'Londoners would be prepared to earn less money in exchange for fulfilment (42% compared to a national average of 36%).' The idea is that a more satisfied employee creates a better workplace and, in turn, enables the social enterprise to be a better business, creating a greater likelihood of prolonged sustainability.

Aristotle viewed happiness as the highest goal of human life. He regarded human happiness as unique, depending on an ability to live virtuously and in accordance with human nature. Professor Paul Whiteley, Director of the Economic Social Research Council

(ESRC) Democracy and Participation Programme (2001–2003), confirmed a correlation between working to help others and contributing to your own happiness. The Economic Social Research Council found that people with strong relationships were likely to be happier and that having a higher self-esteem had the power to transform lives. Professor Whiteley noted that, by focusing on the needs of others, people might also reap benefits themselves and achieve a better quality of life.

Social networks

To make as big a difference as possible, entrepreneurs need to use their skills wisely and effectively. Entrepreneurs kick things off, but they cannot complete the task without help and social networks appear to be a good way of involving other people

Social networks facilitate activities of potential entrepreneurs by introducing them to opportunities, resources and personal contacts. Getting to know the right person in the area or the parent with the relevant contacts can turn an idea into a reality very quickly. Linking up with other local community leaders increases the chances of getting start-up funds for some groups and, in the case of other groups, their work may be actually sustained by a network of social contacts. Social entrepreneurs create assets for the community that would not otherwise exist. It may be in the form of buildings or new services, but the real social capital comes from a network of relationships that underpins economic partnerships and alliances. These networks depend upon a culture of cooperation, fostered by shared values and trust.

Developing new models, social entrepreneurs excel at mobilising a diverse network of people and companies to join forces and come up with joint solutions.

(Leadbeater, 1997, p. 218)

For many people there is very little in today's society that they can feel a part of or believe in. The connections are lost and people are becoming more isolated and fearful. The early years services have a vitally important role to play in helping address this problem, for children and their families and for society as a whole. Leading a social enterprise therefore places a moral, social and economic responsibility on many early years leaders.

To address the issue, it is first necessary to be able to articulate and embed the values of social justice and then consider what can be done to help. Then, the values and vision needs to be woven throughout the whole of the organisation and further beyond. Social entrepreneurship can drive social change and bring lasting transformational benefits to society and communities: better health, lower crime, improved educational performance and greater life satisfaction.

Leadbeater (1997) implied that the social entrepreneur must be pragmatic, opportunistic and visionary but remain realistic about the nature of the problems clients confront. They need to be good at establishing networks, be socially confident and driven by the need to address real problems and capable of dealing with people. They need to be innovative, creating new services and products, finding new ways of dealing with problems, often by bringing together approaches that have traditionally been kept separate. Most importantly, they can transform the neighbourhood and communities they serve by opening up possibilities for self-development.

> *Social entrepreneurs know from hard-won experience that the trick is first to demonstrate what you are proposing to do for people in a small and tangible way and then to expand the sense of possibility.*

(Mawson, 2008, p. 3)

Starting a network

If you want to start an entrepreneurial network for, for example, men in childcare, consider the following key issues.

- Purpose and what you want to achieve from the network

  Ask yourself, do you want:

  - To have national representation?
  - To develop local formal networking opportunities
  - To lobby and influence government and other stakeholders?
  - To promote the concept of men in childcare?
  - To research and develop?
  - To create information sharing with other relevant organisations (such as, in the instance given above, Fatherhood institute or Working with Men)?

- Structure

  What structure do you want to have? Consider:

  - Size
  - Membership
  - Geography
  - Cluster
  - Business support
  - External agency lead.

- Communication

  How will you communicate? Will you have:

  - A directory of members?

- Regular roundtables?
- A website for members (where they can post information such as news, jobs, events, products and services)?
- Sub-groups forming around special interests?
- Newsletters?
- Website links?
- Social media, e.g. Facebook, Twitter, YouTube?
- A helpline?

- Evaluation
How will you enable the network to evaluate what it is doing and whether it is achieving its aims? Check:
- Are members usefully engaged?
- Are there enough meetings?
- Is the membership right for everyone?
- Is there a timetable for reviewing progress?
- Is there direction, coordination and organisation?
- Are the objectives being met?
- Are there enough of the right resources?

Think and reflect!

Check your understanding of whether your organisation is a social enterprise by answering the questions below.

Is your organisation a social enterprise?

1 What do you think constitutes a social enterprise?

2 Why do you think your organisation is a social enterprise?

3 How do the values of your organisation ensure you operate as a social enterprise?

4 Is your business model designed to contribute to community cohesion?

5 What do you do with your profit that will make a difference to children, families, staff, community and society?

6 If your organisation were to become a social enterprise, what changes would you need to make?

Activity to complete at a staff team meeting or training session

The activity is provided to be used at a staff team meeting or training session to provoke discussion and get the staff to think about how they would respond and what skills, knowledge and understanding they would use and why.

Consider the following scenario.

You are the new leader of a charity, sector-run neighbourhood nursery which is now being taken on by LEYF . The local people are suspicious as they have not been consulted or involved in this change. Despite this, you are being tasked to deliver services that contractors tell you the community expected, but were always managed from the head office of the parent charity central services in the local town five miles away from your setting. You now need to deliver a service, derived from people who have their own professional values and ways of working.

There is an obvious lack of understanding of high quality childcare. These are only some of the challenges that need to be overcome. Answer the following questions:

- How will you start and achieve a quick win?
- What enterprising skills will you apply?
- How will you establish what really needs to be done?
- How will you get buy-in from the local community?
- What will you do now, next month and in the future?
- How will you build the plan so it feeds into the self-evaluation form?
- Where will you go for support?

9 Leading with your governors and trustees

Many early years settings might wish to consider reviewing their governance arrangements. Faced with difficult and challenging times resulting from financial cuts, legislative changes and shortage of trustees they might consider different leadership and governance arrangements, such as joining up with a charity and working under one board of trustees, or adapting to a different governance model, such as becoming a community interest company or a social enterprise or cooperative setting. The voluntary sector tends to be governed by a board of trustees also known as a management committee, council or board of directors.

What is governance?

Governance, according to Good Governance; A Code for the Community and Voluntary Sector, is all about the systems and processes concerned with the overall direction, effectiveness, supervision and accountability of an organisation. Governance covers the main aspects of the organisation's purpose. This includes everything that affects the running of the service: strategy, finance, staff, standards, compliance, risk, reputation and how we ensure the organisation is sustainable and operating to meet its purpose.

Although each organisation may have a different profile and make-up, ultimately the status of the organisation and the governance structure is shaped by the Charities Act 2011 and if an organisation is incorporated, then also by the Companies Act 2006. For example, if the charity is in the form of a company, someone under the age of 18 may serve as a director but, for unincorporated bodies and trusts, the trustees must be over 18.

A charity or voluntary organisation is governed by a set of documents called the memorandum and articles. The memorandum lays out the purpose of the organisation and the articles dictate what the board can and cannot do with the funds and the rules for operating. An organisation can only do what its memorandum dictates or that which it is authorised by statute to do. The trustees or board members must operate within this remit and demonstrate how, by acting prudently, they are securing the interests of the organisation so it remains solvent, assets and funds are used wisely and no action is knowingly taken that would place the organisational reputation at undue risk. For example, a trustee must ensure there are clear, robust policies and procedures that ensure the organisation is legal, and they must have a set of financial procedures which are designed to reduce the risk of fraud or misuse of monies. For instance, sometimes a voluntary organisation or charity receives monies for specific purposes, such as a grant to build an extension. Trustees have to know how this restricted money is accounted for so that it is used for that specific purpose only. If a trustee authorised the use of a restricted fund for some other purpose without the funder's consent, they might become personally liable. However, the Charities Act 2011 has made it possible for charities to insure the people who sit on their board. The Act expressly allows the charity to buy trustees indemnity insurance which was formerly a grey area under the Companies Act 2006. It covers them from having to personally pay out when claims are made against them, as long as the mistake was honestly made and not the result of wilful misconduct.

Incorporation of a charity

Organisations are very often charities and companies limited by guarantee. If the organisation is not incorporated, it is worth considering incorporation when the organisation is growing and getting involved in areas which create risks such as signing leases and taking on staff, or when the organisation has grown through an amalgamation with another organisation. Charities can become incorporated in a number of ways.

These include:

- A company limited by guarantee

- An industrial and provident society

- By royal charter

- By statute such as the Charities Act 2011 which allows small charities to incorporate as a Charitable Incorporated Organisation (CIO).

Incorporation gives protection through limited liability. In effect the organisation becomes a corporate person and trustees are the means by which that corporate person makes decisions. Therefore if things go wrong, in most circumstances, it is the organisation against which the claim lies, even if the trustee signed the lease or other document creating the liability.

Incorporated charities are required to register and complete a number of tasks, including filing annual returns, and keeping proper registers of who is a director or company secretary. Failing in these duties may result in a fine or, in extreme cases, imprisonment. Before considering incorporation, examine the organisation's administrative capacity to comply with the registration requirements.

The board of trustees

According to Section 177 of the Charities Act (2011) charity trustees 'means the persons having the general control and management of the administration of a charity.' The board is the body that takes decisions, sets direction and ensures that the work of the organisation is carried out. The board is responsible for the overall governance of the organisation, ensuring compliance with their memorandum and articles and relevant legislation. It is accountable in law.

Members of the board cannot all be experts in everything, so it is a good idea to divide up some of the key tasks between individuals. Some people may have expertise or an interest in a specific area: finance will be the remit of the treasurer, but other areas such as marketing or HR could be the remit of other board members. The chair of trustees acts on behalf of the board of trustees and is accountable to them. No individual trustee, including the chair, has authority unless specifically acting on behalf of the board and with the delegated authority of the board.

Leading with your governors and trustees

Collectively, trustees have authority. Individually they do not, unless acting with written delegated authority from the board as a whole.

Trustees tend to be responsible for the following:

- Anything affecting the registration of the charity or company

- Any changes to be made to the governing documents

- Approving arrangements for dealing with complaints

- Processes and procedures required to further the aims of the charity's memorandum and statutes

- Defining and agreeing the strategic aims and objectives of the organisation

- Financial reporting (e.g. posting accounts or statutory income reports to Companies House and the Charity Commission or whichever is relevant)

- Approving the budget

- Holding an annual general meeting for members, where applicable

- Approving/amending the policies and procedures for internal control and the management of risk

- Agreeing and reviewing the investment strategy, in line with relevant policies

- Ensuring that trading and other activities do not compromise the organisation's charitable status

- Agreeing changes to the staff's pension scheme or the management of its funds

- Appointing the external auditors

- Establishing/reviewing/amending/approving key organisational policies

- Appointing honorary officers

- Agreeing sub-committee members
- Delegation of powers from the board to sub-committees and their terms of reference
- Agreeing a system for reimbursing trustee expenses or/and remuneration
- Declaraing trustee interests that may conflict with those of the organisation
- Recruiting new board members
- Evaluating the board's progress
- Appointing, appraising and dismissing the chief executive officer
- Approving/rejecting proposals regarding the salary and benefits of the chief executive and other senior management, where appropriate
- Reviewing progress of the organisation.

Honorary roles

Honorary officers play an important role in helping the board work effectively. They are ordinary trustees selected by the board and given limited powers to act on the board's behalf. They commonly include chairs, vice-chairs, treasurers and secretaries. The duties of honorary officers vary depending on the size of the organisation. For example, in a very small organisation the treasurer may be involved in everything from managing accounts to budgeting, but in a larger organisation this work will be done by qualified finance staff. It helps if the honorary officers have a written role description and special training in their role, if necessary.

Reviewing the board

Greater Manchester Centre for Voluntary Organisation (GMCVO) listed their 12 essential trustee board roles, which are clear and succinct. These are useful when reviewing the effectiveness of the board.

1 Set and maintain vision, mission and values

2 Develop strategy

3 Establish and monitor policies

4 Ensure reliable employment procedures. The trustee board checks the organisation has comprehensive, fair and legal personnel policies. These protect the organisation and those who work for it. They cover:

- Recruitment
- Support

- Appraisal
- Remuneration
- Discipline

5. It also recruits and selects new trustee board members

6. Ensures compliance to governing documents

7. Ensures accountability

8. Ensures compliance with the law

9. Maintains proper fiscal oversight

10. Selects and supports the chief executive

11. Respects the role of staff

12. Maintains effective board performance.

Successful boards

Generally, board members need to be constructive and supportive and clear as to why they are trustees and what their role is in supporting the management in order to make the organisation a success. In my view a successful board balances its responsibility with that of the management and knows its role and responsibilities. Getting the right information makes this possible. The chance of trustees asking the right questions to get the best information is greater when the board members have the right balance of skills and experience, take an interest in the organisational core business and have opportunities to learn about the organisation's purpose and the sector and market in which it is operating.

A good chair runs a good meeting and manages the board so the trustees are all working together with management for the best interests of the organisation. If there are sub-committees, they need to be formed to add value and improve governance and so be relevant. Sub-committees are often organised to support major issues such as remuneration or major building works. Otherwise, managers should be able to call on trustees for advice to help them make decisions. A good chair helps foster effective communication so the expectations of everyone are clear. In these days of email, it is easy to get overwhelmed by information and requests and it can lead to confusion.

Boards have to help management balance risk and innovation so the organisation can react to new experiences and be able to continually move forward without risking the core business. Finally, a good board has a great role to play in supporting the staff and giving praise where it is due as well as believing in and promoting the organisation.

Company directors

Some charities and voluntary organisations are also registered as companies, which means that the trustees are also company directors. Company directors have a series of duties very similar to those of trustees. Like trustee duties, these come with being a director of an incorporated body and can carry personal liability. These duties can be summarised as follows:

- Duty to act within the powers of the governing document
- Duty to promote the success of the company but have regard to other factors such as the consequences for employees
- Duty to exercise independent judgement
- Duty to exercise reasonable care, skill and diligence – this means not just being careful, but using the general knowledge, skill and experience that would be reasonably expected of someone carrying out such functions as well as using relevant and specific skills or knowledge
- Duty to avoid conflicts of interest
- Duty not to accept benefits from third parties by reason of being a director
- Duty to declare an interest in any proposed transaction or arrangements
- Duty to promote the success of the company.

The role of the chair

The board delegates the responsibility to run the organisation to the head, and the chair runs the board. Often the chair is the person delegated to support the chief executive, director or CEO, or whatever the person in charge of the organisation is called. Some chairs will conduct an annual appraisal. The relationship between the chair and the CEO is very important and good quality communication and dialogue is critical between the two of them so they know what is going on. Their relationship needs to be balanced. If there is no support and and there is constant challenge, then either person, or both, will feel beleaguered and defensive and give up. If it is too cosy, there is a risk of complacency and things could slip. Governing bodies led by an effective chair can support the CEO by providing clarity, support, consistency and feedback.

The chair's job is to set the agenda for the meeting with the head of service to ensure trustees get the right balance of information in terms of briefing, papers and presentations. Trustees need information that is meaningful. The right information will provide context and confidence which, in turn, offers reassurance and enables trustees to make proper decisions in order to assure compliance and financial integrity, and meet governance responsibilities.

A good chair

Below is a list of the characteristics of a good chair. It is useful when reviewing personal or organisational competence. A good chair:

- Cares about the cause
- Stimulates new thinking
- Gives support when needed
- Has a clear understanding of the different roles
- Does not interfere constantly
- Has experience of leading a complex organisation
- Is not just there for personal ambition
- Has the respect of the board
- Has a sense of humour
- Has strength of character to question the leader in a way that no one else in the organisation will
- Respects the leader and is respected by the leader
- Is good at chairing meetings and encourages full cooperation
- Has a network of contacts to bring to the organisation.

Parent Council

The Education and Inspections Act 2006 places a duty on governing bodies of all maintained schools to take account of the views expressed by parents of registered pupils. All settings are encouraged to review their arrangements for listening to parents and to consider enhancing them by setting up a Parent Council. Ofsted inspects settings on the way in which they listen and respond to parents' views in the judgement on leadership and management.

These parent bodies are run by parents, giving them an independent voice in schools and enhancing their involvement and participation across the school. The Parent Council's role is advisory and consultative. It plays an important role in informing decision-making processes but it cannot make decisions on behalf of the school. The governors are responsible for ensuring that the purpose of the Parent Council is clear to all school parents and teachers and that there is a shared understanding of how it will work. Some schools may decide to appoint a working group to take responsibility for establishing and running the Parent Council and to review and evaluate its effectiveness over time. The head teacher is expected to liaise with the Parent Council, providing support and information, responding to ideas and suggestions and taking issues forward through the right channels.

Trustee committee

Most governing documents such as memoranda and articles allow the board of trustees to designate authority to another group of trustees to review and agree areas of development. Some charities have fixed sub-committees such as finance and internal audit. Others have committees that fit their core business or largest source of expenditure, such as facilities/properties and staff, and others have opportunities for short-term committees which reflect areas of development or change that need some attention; for example, a remuneration committee to oversee the re-evaluation of jobs and salaries.

The secret of successful committees is to have a proper approval process with clear roles and task definition, shared communication and adequate monitoring. It is a good idea to have written terms of reference which clarify what is being delegated, the decision-making power and the staff roles in relation to the committee. The reporting process is also critical, particularly in terms of minutes and feeding back to the main board. For example, agreeing whether committee minutes are sent to all trustees for information in advance of a board meeting, as part of the board papers or whether there is an oral feedback at each board meeting from the chairs of the committees. It is very important that the board chair and the committee chair /leader agree the process to avoid contradiction and confusion and to reduce the chance of feeling foolish at the board meeting. However, no matter what work is delegated, the board as a whole is equally and jointly responsible for making decisions for the organisation.

The board needs to monitor the work of committees, regularly reviewing their roles to make sure they are still serving a purpose. No committee should be allowed to usurp the board's decision-making authority by taking decisions without proper authority.

Possible terms of reference for a committee

Different committees generally have different terms of reference. However, you may find it useful to consider the following.

Does the committee have:

- A clear description of the work?
- Authority to make decisions?
- A schedule that fits with the board meeting so the two dovetail together?
- Reporting requirements?
- Details of committee membership?

- Budget and spending authority?
- A review date?

The role of the early years leader

Governance states that the role of the leader of the organisation, whether called a director, chief executive, head teacher or managing director, is to lead, manage and administer the organisation within the strategic and accountability frameworks laid down by the board. Some boards are very formal, others are more involved in operational business because of the limited resources of the organisation. As a leader it is necessary to understand the requirements of your board as it is fundamental to a successful and positive relationship.

Together with the chair, the director, chief executive, CEO, or whatever your leadership title, enables the board to fulfil its duties and responsibilities for the proper governance of the organisation and ensures that the board receives timely advice and appropriate information on all relevant matters. For example, the head of a children's centre will work with the governors to develop a shared vision and strategy for the centre. Governance is about ensuring the organisation is lawful, well managed and financially viable and trustees need the kind of information that will help them implement this. Therefore, on a practical basis, I have found the structures listed below to be helpful.

An annual meeting plan

Use the financial cycle to help plan meetings so that all the important financial information is collected and ready for the board meeting for approval, discussion or signing off. This includes:

- Quarterly accounts
- End-of-year accounts
- Budget and reforecast dates
- Auditor's visit and report
- Internal audit to check internal systems are working
- Strategic planning (an away day or whatever means you use to involve trustees in agreeing the next set of objectives).

Get the cycle of meetings right so there is a rationale for every meeting. Sometimes there is a system already in place that does not work and the meeting schedule is illogical for the needs of the organisation and trustees never get the right information at the right time.

Board meetings

Put the relevant issues on the agenda. These are all the areas for which trustees are responsible. This includes finance, staff, health and safety, compliance and risk. It is usual to also have something that shows progress against strategic objectives; for example, presenting the business plan twice a year. Trustees have an obligation to sign off the strategy, key policies and procedures and significant financial decisions. Each organisation is different, but issues of concern should always feature on the agenda or in the leader's report, such as occupancy, repayment of debt, complaints or other factors that matter to the organisation and is critical to success.

One-to-one with the chair

It is a good idea for the leader to meet the chair before the board meeting. This is the time to plan what is happening in the organisation and to discuss new challenges, opportunities and threats. Testing the water with the chair first is very helpful. A good chair will also help you work out how to present these issues to the board, for example, in the form of a PowerPoint presentation, a paper, a tabled item for discussion or delegated to a committee. Such a plan means the necessary decisions can be made and signed off and the leader has the backing of the board to progress.

In terms of the annual away day, planning this with the chair is crucial so there is a shared approach and the right information is gathered in advance. Away days can be more effective when facilitated by an external person. It means the chair and the leader have time to fully participate in the process without having to either chair or minute the proceedings.

A good chair will help set personal goals and targets for the leader. Some chairs recommend mentoring for the leader as a means of support and independent personal development. It is certainly worth thinking about because being at the top is lonely and stressful and having a neutral ear can only add value. Choosing the right person is very important as the chair and the organisational leader need to be in tune.

Conflict with the board

Sadly, there can be conflict between the organisational leader and the trustees. It mostly comes down to a failure to understand each other's roles and the collision of governance with management. It can be reduced by having a good relationship with the chair. Sometimes the conflict comes from poor communication or a particular attitude that neither really understand nor can articulate. Trustees are people and consequently have their idiosyncratic ways which it takes time to understand. Leaders themselves are equally idiosyncratic and can also be egotistical and resent having their wings clipped by trustees. Other factors, such as the process of making decisions through boards, can be long-winded and frustrating, which can cause conflict. Time is not always available to a leader trying to manage complex external factors and the governance processes may add to the stress and cause tension.

Understanding the role of governance is critical, as well as preparing papers which give enough information to help trustees make decisions. Keeping communication as open and informative as possible is very important. However, if there is conflict, getting external help to resolve the matter quickly is worth consideration.

Liabilities of staff and volunteers

As soon as an organisation moves from being a purely voluntary body to employing staff, the level of risk that it faces goes up substantially. The organisation, whether incorporated or not, owes its volunteers and staff a duty of care. These responsibilities are complex and rapidly changing. Key duties to staff, and therefore liabilities, include:

- Financial obligations which include salary, pension, holiday and redundancy pay

- Procedural duties, the need to provide disciplinary, grievance and other appropriate procedures

- The obligation to provide a contract or terms and conditions of employment setting out required statutory information

- Insurance requirements, not only the need to meet the statutory required employer's insurance but also to consider a range of other insurances such as personal injury cover

- Duties of care, particularly under health and safety legislation

- Equal opportunities obligations so as not to discriminate on the basis of race, sex, age, religion or disability

- A variety of other statutory obligations, for example, not employing workers who do not have the right to work in this country.

Avoiding problems

The key to avoiding these liabilities is to monitor organisational systems. Some organisations have an internal audit process, when once or twice a year there is a review of all the organisational processes to see if key areas of the organisation are operating effectively. An internal audit can include finance, risk, compliance, health and safety, staffing and complaints. Each organisation has to develop its own system depending on the core business but all internal audits should feature finance.

In addition to an internal audit, employing an external auditor once a year is money well spent. Some organisations with a turnover of less than £100,000 do not have to have an external audit, but I would be very reluctant to avoid a means of checking financial processes. An external audit is a review of what happened in the past and, while it does not lessen a future risk of insolvency, it can flag up weaknesses in the system. The auditor will want to see good budgeting, cash flow projections and monitoring, all of which are key to understanding financial solvency.

Trustees should:

- Ensure that they receive regular, up-to-date financial reports
- Understand the financial position
- Take advice if there are any issues that are not clear to them
- Take advice from their solicitor or accountant if they think insolvency may be a risk.

Who enforces liability?

Breach of these trustee duties could be enforced:

- By the Charity Commission or court – for example ordering the return of income received by an employed trustee
- By the charity itself, for example to recover money lost by an imprudent investment authorised by a trustee
- By the criminal courts, for example a prosecution for misuse of funds.

Conflict of interest

An organisation's most valuable asset is its good name. Trustees are required to bear this in mind at all times and to always act in the best interests of the organisation. All other loyalties must be put to one side. Conflicts of interest can also occur outside the board; for example, between patrons, staff and family members, partners or friends of the trustees, patrons and staff. Therefore, if there is an issue of, say, accepting money from a donor who had a criminal history and taking money from a company associated with bad practice then do the *Sun* headline test. How would the story look if it hit the headlines?

Design a conflict-of-interest form and get trustees to complete one every year. It is quite a good idea to get senior staff, or anyone likely to be representing the organisation or making high-level decisions, to complete one also.

Managing organisational liabilities

The key tools for managing organisational liabilities include:

- Solid processes such as anti-fraud mechanisms, conflict of interest declarations, etc.
- Building financial reserves

- Risk management

- Taking professional advice

- Correct insurance

- Seeking Charity Commission or Court relief

- Knowing and regularly reviewing the governing document to ensure it contains the widest permitted indemnity provision.

Disqualified trustees

Under the Charities Act 2011 and the Companies Act 2006, a person is disqualified from acting as a charity trustee if they:

- Have a conviction for an offence of dishonesty or deception, unless the conviction has been 'spent' under the terms of the Rehabilitation of Offenders Act 1974

- Are bankrupt or have had assets sequestered, unless it has been discharged or permission has been granted under the Disqualification Act 1986

- Have financial problems, meaning they have made a composition or arrangement with creditors under the Insolvency Act 1986 and this has not been discharged

- Have been removed by the Charity Commission, High Court or the Court of Sessions in Scotland from being involved in the management of, or acting as a trustee of, a charitable body

- Have been disqualified under the Company Directors Disqualification Act

- Are subject to an order under the Insolvency Act 1986 for failure to make a payment under a court order.

A disqualified person can apply to the Charity Commission to waive the disqualification. It is a very serious offence to serve without a waiver and is punishable by a fine or up to two years' imprisonment (Charities Act 2011). The Commission can require the repayment of any payments or expenses received while serving as a disqualified trustee.

Recruiting new trustees

The best boards have a broad range of people with the appropriate skills who are all working together to benefit the organisation. This is much the same as most teams. However, many people these days are short of time and more anxious about litigation. Potential trustees, therefore, often need to be persuaded to volunteer their time as well as accepting the responsibility for governing an organisation. Having lots of useful information and designing an induction pack helps them to make a decision. There are a number of different ways of recruiting new trustees. Some organisations use a recruitment agency, some use a charity such as REACH, which looks for trustees for other charities. Others advertise in the main broadsheets or in finance and law magazines. Some managers in local authorities, civil services and large corporations encourage their staff to volunteer as a way of developing their skills and knowledge or through sharing their expertise as a form of their corporate social responsibility agenda.

Whatever route is agreed, think about how you will actually recruit. For example, applicants may be asked for CVs and a supporting statement first, followed by an interview with you and the chair. You may get the agency to recruit first, followed by an interview. Alternatively, you may do a three-pronged approach: the applicant's CV is circulated to everyone; if no trustee objects to the applicant, leader and the chair meet the candidate; and then a final panel of other trustees meet the candidate. Think carefully, make the system work. What is needed is a trustee who will help, be constructive and supportive and who 'gets' what you and the organisation are about. Appointing the wrong trustee is like appointing the wrong staff member: the whole organisation can be affected.

Induction packs

There is much research that says having an induction pack really helps a new trustee understand the organisation and the part they can play in helping contribute. Below is a list of what you might consider including in the induction pack.

- Brief summary of the history of the organisation and mission statement
- Memorandum and articles of association or other constitutional documents
- Details of any sub-committees and their terms of reference
- Detail of any other delegation, e.g. powers to offices
- Charity Commission leaflets, in particular:
    - Responsibilities of a Charity Trustee
    - Hallmarks of an Effective Charity
    - www.charity-commission.gov.uk
- Minutes of previous trustee meetings and sub-committees
- Current strategic plan, cash flow projection and budget
- Most recent management accounts
- Last annual report
- Copy of last risk management report
- Relevant policies

- Contact details for all other trustees and results of last skill audit
- Organisational chart and full details and job descriptions for key staff and details of other staff
- Copies of any existing publications, research documents and other background information
- Job description for trustees
- Trustee Code of Conduct – forms for declaration of interests
- Expense claim forms and information
- List of upcoming events including dates of trustee and sub-committee meetings.

Finally, understanding governance and making it work successfully is very likely to become one of your tasks as an early years leader, if it is not already. Being prepared and finding out about governance early on is sensible and shows considerable foresight. It is also a good investment of time and confirms your understanding that a good leader is prepared and ready to take on new challenges and new ways of doing things. The Department for Education and Skills response to the 'Third Annual Evaluation Report of Academies' (2006) found that, where governance had been reshaped in line with the new structures of academies, there needed to be a way of sharing good practice and establishing networking between governing bodies to both support and challenge the range of governance models available and the types of issues facing governing bodies.

The checklist on the following page is designed for an organisation of any size. It is a means of checking that there is process in place for ensuring governance is robust and the organisation is operating as a business. Don't think that because the organisation is small or funded by the local authority that you don't need to worry about governance and the business structure of the organisation. What is needed is to be sure about the organisational structure and how the plans will be implemented successfully, on a long-term basis. The world is littered with organisations that have failed because they have not considered the business structure and got the basics right. This is critical and it is no good saying 'I did not come into the job to run a business and worry about money'. If you want the organisation to survive so you can continue to make a difference to your children, families and local community, then you have to understand the business structure of your organisation.

Think and reflect!

The checklist has been completed by a hypothetical leader. Have a go at answering the questions in the first column and use the 'Really? Show me the evidence' and 'Now what do you need to do?' columns as a means of assessment.

Board members governance checklist

Governance area	Really? Show me the evidence	Now what do you need to do?
Do you know the values of your organisation?	Yes, I can recite them and they are written in our induction information.	I must check if everyone else gets it.
Is the overall purpose and vision of your organisation clear?	It is written everywhere and staff seem to understand it.	I should check parents and stakeholders get it as well.
Do you have a clear sense of direction for the next few years? Is this communicated across the organisation?	Given the changing times, I probably need to do this again. We need to have a strategy day and use that to refine the direction.	I will present it at the staff conference. Staff surveys indicate this is one of their favourite places to get the information.
How did you involve staff in the process of agreeing future strategy?	I held workshops at the staff conference and hadslots at all key meetings. I gave postcards to each member of staff and noted it on their payslips.	I must ensure more staff involvement and use the pay slips more often.
What information did you use from others involved in the organisation including children, parents and funders?	I used their feedback to add to the strategy and to inform staff about trustee perspectives.	Nothing, I think this has worked well.
Do you have a written plan? Is it useful and relevant?	I have it in my head constantly, although I do look at it before all senior meetings.	I must ensure that senior staff are linking the plan into their departmental reviews.
Do you look at the strategic issues facing the organisation at board meetings?	Yes, but it's not always successful as different board members have a different grasp of the context and there can be a bit of panic.	I should make the issues more explicit.
What systems of checks and balances are in place?	Policy and procedure reviews. Critical incident reviews. Business risk matrix. Due diligence for health and safety. Internal audits to check finance procedures in place. Conflict of interest procedures.	I must keep reading and checking what others do, so we are always learning about ways to mitigate risk.

Governance area	Really? Show me the evidence	Now what do you need to do?
Do you keep up to date with developments and trends in the sector, so as to reduce risk and be better informed?	Yes and I access the most useful magazines. I also attend a couple of key conferences every year.	I must keep on learning.
Has the organisation got the appropriate policies and procedures in place?	Yes.	I must ensure the review timeline is working and agree a signing off process.
Do you have a clear set of guidelines for the decision-making process?	Generally yes, but we have to balance this with common sense and an ability to respond flexibly to new and unknown situations. Communication policy outlines information sharing process.	I must make a chart which states which decisions need trustees' sign off. Keep it with the report template for board meetings as an aide-mémoire so it goes in the papers on time and in the right format to get the decision agreed and signed off.
Does the board get the right information to review progress and make decisions?	The data protection policy states what information should be shared, how much and with whom, as well as how much should be interpreted so as to shape the decision-making process.	I must make sure to apply them as and when needed.
Do the accounts comply with the Charities Act 2006 and Companies Act 2006?	Yes, we have an external audit every year. It's worth the money for the piece of mind.	I must keep an eye on changes as there are some coming imminently.
Do you keep proper books and records of all transactions?	Yes, we use software to do this and keep a register of assets also.	I must keep them up to date.
Do you have a finance sub-committee? How often do they meet?	Yes, four times a year.	I should ensure they always get the right information such as quarterly management accounts.
Is there a business risk assessment in place and a set of review dates?	Yes.	In the light of the recession, I need to review this again.

Governance area	Really? Show me the evidence	Now what do you need to do?
How often do trustees review your income and expenditure against your budget?	We have monthly accounts which give very helpful information. These accounts form the basis of our three monthly reports to trustees on the finance committee.	I must keep on track.
Do you have an asset register?	Yes	I must keep it up to date.
Does the board regularly check and approve the management accounts?	Yes, draft minutes from the finance sub-committee are approved by the full board. Everyone gets the minutes.	No change is required as the system works.
Do you have a system for internal and external audits?	Yes	I must make sure the internal audits are checking all the financial procedures.
Is there clear leadership? Is there a strong sense of commitment to shared set of values and ethos?	The chair and the chief executive have a positive working relationship and work closely to ensure the strategy and organisation development is in line with the values of the organisation. The board can challenge this at the meetings.	I should arrange the annual trustee away day and get a facilitator who can ensure we check this.
Is there a clear staffing structure and lines of responsibility?	Yes we have a chart.	I must keep it updated.
What systems are in place for communication across the organisation?	We have a communication policy which identifies how we share information and how we use best practice to ensure it is effective.	I must update the website. It is a wasted facility at the moment.

Activity to complete at an away day or training session

The activity is provided to be used at an away day or training session as a means to measure yourselves against the following grade descriptors for leading and managing an outstanding school.

Show how you, as a board of governors, help to ensure :

- The pursuit of excellence in all of the school's activities is demonstrated by an uncompromising and highly successful drive to strongly improve, or maintain, the highest levels of achievement and personal development for all pupils over a sustained period of time.

- All leaders and managers, including those responsible for governance, are highly ambitious for the pupils and lead by example. They base their actions on a deep and accurate understanding of the school's performance and of staff and pupils' skills and attributes.

- Governors, or those with a similar responsibility, stringently hold senior leaders to account for all aspects of the school's performance.

- Excellent policies underpin practice that ensures that pupils have high levels of literacy, or pupils are making excellent progress in literacy.

- Leaders focus relentlessly on improving teaching and learning and provide focused professional development for all staff, especially those that are newly qualified and at an early stage of their careers. This is underpinned by searching performance management that encourages, challenges and supports teachers' improvement. As a result, the overall quality of teaching is at least consistently good and improving.

- The school's curriculum promotes and sustains a thirst for knowledge and understanding and a love of learning. It covers a wide range of subjects and provides opportunities for academic, technical and sporting excellence. It has a very positive impact on all pupils' behaviour and safety, and contributes very well to pupils' academic achievement, their physical well-being, and their spiritual, moral, social and cultural development.

- The school's actions have secured improvement in achievement for disadvantaged pupils, which is rising rapidly, including in English and mathematics.

- The school has highly successful strategies for engaging with parents to the benefit of pupils, including those who find working with the school difficult.

- Senior leaders in the school work to promote improvement across the wider system including, where applicable, with early years providers to raise the proportion of children who are well prepared to start school.

- The school is adept at identifying any child at risk of harm and engaging with partners to respond appropriately. Staff model professional standards in all of their work and demonstrate high levels of respect and courtesy for pupils and others.

- Through highly effective, rigorous planning and controls, governors ensure financial stability, including the effective and efficient management of financial resources such as the pupil premium funding. This leads to the excellent deployment of staff and resources to the benefit of all groups of pupils.

- Leaders have ensured that early years and/or sixth form provision is highly effective.

10 Leading the way forward

Nowadays, leadership is connected with the future. Leaders are forward-looking, not just responding to today's issues but considering tomorrow's opportunities. They are looking ahead, thinking about the next steps, imagining what difference they can make and how they can make the ordinary extraordinary. Noel Tichy (2004) believed that winning leaders create and use future stories to help people break away from the familiar present and venture boldly ahead to create a better future. They not only describe the future in terms that are personal and compelling but they help others understand why and what they must do to get there. Good leaders need to be able to tell the story about the next journey to be undertaken. They often describe this as 'the vision', because the vision is the picture of the future and how leaders can take their organisation forward in a way that will guarantee they continue to make a difference.

For many people just thinking about the future scares them, because it implies change and this can be terrifying, even if it is a change for the good, a change to ensure survival. People are much more comfortable clinging to what they know and can understand. A leader is able to bring people through this journey of anxiety and nervousness and, therefore, needs to be brave and take the first step showing courage and conviction. Nothing gains the respect of others more quickly than when they see their leader taking the first steps into the unknown and being prepared to lead.

Powerful leadership traits

Leadership remains an important topic in the early years. The connection has been made between a good leader and a successful leader. For future leaders there is some help as the consensus about what leaders need to know, be able to do and understand to make that difference, is confirmed.

There are common themes emerging throughout this book that intimate leadership success. The most prominent appear to include the ability to articulate the philosophy, particularly a pedagogical philosophy, which underpins everything leaders do and want to achieve. It sets up a leader as a culture setter, creating a culture of support, success and acceptance in the organisation and building a structure around this so the core values are absorbed, implemented and embedded at every level of the organisation. This becomes more and more critical the bigger the organisation becomes and the further away the leader gets from the real business. This takes us to the next important feature of leadership: the ability to grow leaders within the organisation and support them so that throughout the organisation there is a culture of support, development, growth and praise.

One of the features of successful leadership which I think is critical, especially in the fast-changing world of working with children, is the ability to be a creative thinker and keep things fresh and fun in the organisation. This is not an easy task,but an organisation cannot be allowed to go stale. Creative leaders develop the means of getting people to look at things differently and push boundaries. In doing this, they get people to accept change as a given and realise that change is a natural process, not a major hurdle, and best achieved when the organisation is flexible and responsive and copes with, and manages, change as a normal course of action.

The concept of emotional intelligence is, to my mind, fundamental to success, both in terms of personal survival and winning the respect of staff, colleagues and customers. Emotional intelligence is the ability to read a situation and use a personal antennae to understand all the nuances and dynamics that ripple through human interactions and relationships. It is also about being able to read the politics of the situation. This is particularly critical in terms of networking, representation and developing partnerships. Leaders with emotional intelligence tend to be better listeners, and demonstrate an ability to step into someone else's shoes and generally respond with heightened sensitivity, therefore reducing conflict, miscommunication and de-motivation.

Running an early years setting, no matter what the shape, size or structure, requires an ability to convert the philosophy into practical application and solve problems as they arise and, where possible, before they arise. It is about being pragmatic and getting things done while remaining flexible and adaptable. Children's settings need to balance calm and order with opportunities for versatility and this is much more successful when the structure is stable. Children are gloriously anarchic and managing their anarchy, in a way that captures the best aspects of it, is a great ability and creates a fantastic environment.

Ultimately leadership is also about being responsible, accountable and taking the role seriously. It is about humility as leaders realise that people have entrusted them with the power associated with the role. Leaders can make a positive difference in so many ways. As John Quincy Adams, the second president of the United States once said:

If your actions inspire others to dream more, learn more, do more and become more, you are a leader.

(John Quincy Adams, 1767–1848)

I am constantly humbled when I think about how so many people entrust their children to those of us working as leaders in early years settings, believing in our ability to lead an organisation successfully so their children have the best care and education. Responsible leaders keep learning. Staff respect leaders who know more than them, who can guide them and who are willing to enter into new ways of thinking and, in doing so, produce an atmosphere of continual quality improvement where staff are valued as competent and capable learners and teachers.

Continual challenges

There is no doubt that the early years sector faces a future of more change and challenges. This means that leaders need to be constantly reflecting on their own performance and checking if they have the right skills and support needed to meet the changing demands.

More and more emphasis is being placed on the leader's ability to connect, network, make relationships and develop partnerships. This is all set against a background of the standard leadership challenges, such as competition, fragmentation of services and funding crises.

There is great pressure on today's early years leaders in all sectors to develop inter-agency approaches and inter-generational services. Leaders have an increasingly important role to play to improve collaboration between groups of schools, children's centres and other agencies in order to provide inclusive and sustainable extended services. This approach is more beneficial to families and communities, especially families who access a number of services or who have many problems. No one would refute that this is a logical and sensible way forward, but its complexity is often denied.

Making this happen is a huge challenge to leaders, especially when trying to bring services together. Leaders are often faced with having to address an age-old problem of incongruity in values and organisational behaviour. This is not an insurmountable problem and leaders who have a clear philosophy and can articulate their position are often better placed to form partnerships because they understand how their values will align with those of another organisation. It is when there is uncertainty and confusion that anxieties increase and people shut down. To be able to share work practices and encourage and develop partnerships you need to be mature and confident, given the potential risks to things going awry, including reputational risk and loss of funds. However, the benefits are also great, in that once the partnership is formed there are greater opportunities for new ways of making things better for children and their families. In my experience, staying put is neither helpful nor sensible.

Modern leaders are encouraged to network as well as creating networks. Networking involves going to events and making links, in some ways lobbying, while creating networks requires the ability to find interested organisations and connect them. There is a need for practitioner-led networks where staff can get some peer support. I think networks are particularly useful for new leaders and those keen to become leaders, especially if they can discuss practical situations. Networks can be a useful means of developing practitioners as leaders and reflectors and can also encourage action research. Networks can also be a place where questions can be posed and a whole range of responses identified and tested. Networks are an exciting option. Networks are not the same as networking. Leaders need to do this as well, no matter how much you hate making small talk or understanding politics. Invest time and effort in networking. It can take many forms and is the best way to raise the organisational profile.

Remember to:

- Promote your organisation enthusiastically wherever you go
- Put in time with your contacts outside the business – invite them for lunch, go to events
- Spend time talking to professionals in the sector – let them know you exist
- Get to know some journalists
- Build alliances by cooperating, even in small ways, with other organisations.

Today all leaders face an economic storm and this can be a steep learning curve for many. The word 'recession' gets people very worried and the board of governors could be feeling very nervous. Decisions regarding organisational sustainability are even more critical, especially where the margin for mistakes is very narrow. As a leader, you need to guide the board and help them resist making strategic decisions which could be regretted later. For example, a classic management reaction to recession is to put training and career development on hold. In fact, this is a good time to develop in-house training options in areas such as leadership, motivation and how you add value to what you do (sometimes known as impact measurement). In bad times, rumours can become magnified, so communication is critical and honesty is the best policy. In hard times, the leader needs to be strong and keep morale high. Hard times are a real test for a leader because it is much easier to be a leader when the good times roll.

Today we are bombarded with information. It is hard to find a quiet moment. However, to lead it is essential to have time to think. Ideas are hard to find when there is no clear space. Most leaders have their best ideas almost anywhere other than in the office. I often get my best ideas travelling on long train journeys. Take a walk and use opportunities to get in contact with people. Ideas are sparked off through conversations, visits to other settings, seminars, daydreaming, listening to the radio, watching television, reading books and magazines, visiting website, links and blogs, a chance remark in the most unlikely circumstances, if your mind is open to receive these ideas. I often wake in the night and now I keep post-it notes by my bed to scribble down what seems a coherent idea at the time, but can be hard to remember properly in the morning. Whatever you decide to do, give yourself, and all the leaders you are developing and supporting, thinking time so they can cogitate and consider and come up with imaginative and original ideas, solutions and better ways of doing things.

Finally, leaders in early years need to be constantly alert to quality and the business of giving every child the best start. Public expectations have risen regarding the care and educational contributions of early years settings to children's future development. This expectation is aligned with increased research which reminds us that our contribution is significant and we cannot afford to get it wrong. Sadly, many settings are still mediocre and not at all inspiring. Too many staff are poorly trained, unsupported or left to their own devices. Leaders must shoulder this problem and address it no matter what the pain. We have to campaign for what is good for children. We must behave intelligently and debate the benefits and limitations of policy initiatives and always strive to put our words into action and create the type of service that will help narrow the achievement gap between children.

The role of the leader is critical and must remain in the front of people's minds. Leaders need to remember the authority they hold. Our passion for making a difference must inspire the present and future leaders in the sector. Helen Keller (1880–1968) said that life was either a daring adventure or nothing. We must be brave and have the courage of our convictions. In other words:

- Be passionate, believe in what you do
- Be 'out there'
- Lead from where staff can see
- Set a good example
- Think, think, think
- Communicate
- Give context and meaning
- Take responsibility
- Be accountable
- Make it happen
- Persevere and have patience
- Relax and reward yourself for a job well done.

Bibliography

Adair, J. (2002) *Inspiring Leadership*. London: Thorogood.

Adair, J. (2005) *The Inspirational Leader*. London: Kogan and Page.

Adams, J. Q. (1767–1848) www.quotationspage.com, accessed 24.01.09.

Ahmed, M. (2008) 'End shortermism demands Action for Children', *Community Care*, 18 September

Aubrey, C. (2007) *Leading and Managing in the Early Years*. London: Sage Publication.

Battle, M. (1997) *Reconciliation*. Cleveland, OH: Pilgrim Press.

Bradley, J. (2007), 'Social entrepreneurship: the case for definition', Stanford Social Innovation Review. www.ssireview.org/articles/socialentrepreneurship, accessed from website 29/05/09.

Belsky, J. and Vondra, J. (1989) 'Understanding the causes of neglect', www.2009eNotAlone.com, accessed 7.02.09.

Bennett, N., Harvey, J. A., Wise, C. and Woods, P. A. (2003) *Distributed Leadership: A Desk Study* www.ncsl.org.uk/literaturereviews, accessed 5.12.08.

Bennis, W. (1992) *On Becoming a Leader*. London: Addison-Wesley.

Bhabra, S. and Ghate, D. (2004) *Parent Information Point: Evaluation of the Pilot Phase*. UK: National Family and Parenting Institute.

Bird, J. (2007) *How to Change Your Life in 7 Steps*. London: Vermilion.

Bottery, M. (2004) *The Challenges of Educational Leadership*. London: Paul Chapman Publishing.

Bradley, J. (2007) *Social Entrepreneurship: The Case for Definition – Social Enterprise: A Definition. US*. Stanford, CT: Social Innovation Review.

Bronfenbrenner, U. (1979) *The Ecology of Human Development: Experiments by Nature and Design*. Cambridge, MA: Harvard University Press.

Buckingham, M. and Coffman, C. (1999) *Break All the Rules*. London: Simon & Shuster.

Budget Speech 1997, HM Treasury, www.archive.treasury.gov.uk, accessed 10.02.09.

Championing Children (2006) *Championing Children: A Shared Set of Skills, Knowledge and Behaviours for Those Leading and Managing Integrating Children's Services* (2nd edition). Nottingham: DfES Publications.

Championing Children (2007) *Resource Book Championing Children: A Shared Set of Skills, Knowledge and Behaviours for Those Leading and Managing Integrating Children's Services* CWDC March 2007.

Children Act 1998 and 2004. London: HMSO.

Children's Workforce Development Council (2008) *Building Brighter Futures: Next Steps for the Children's Workforce*. Nottingham: Department Children Schools Families Publications.

Cleveland, H. (2002) 'Leadership: the get it all together profession', *The Futurist*, Sept.–Oct, pp. 42–7.

Cohen, B. and Greenfield, J. (1997) *How to Run a Value Led Business and Make Money Too*. (First Fireside edition). New York: Simon & Schuster Inc.

Cotter, N. (2004) 'Adapting authentic leadership', *The Training Zone*, November, Oct. 2004.

Day, C. (2005) 'The passion of successful leadership', *School Leadership and Management*, 24(4): 425–37.

Deakins, D. (1996) *Entrepreneurship and Small Firms*. London: McGraw Hill.

Dearing, E. McCartney, K. and Taylor, B. (2004) 'Change in family income-to-needs matters more for children with less', in NICHD [National Institute of Child Health and Human Development] Early Child Care Research Network (eds) *Child Care and Child Development: Results from the NICHD Study of Early Child Care and Youth Development*. New York: Guilford Publications.

Desforges, C. and Abouchaar, A. (2003) *The Impact of Parental Involvement and Family Education on Pupil Achievement and Adjustment: A Literature Review*. Research Department 433, London, Department of Education and Skills.

Ebbeck, M. and Waniganayake, M. (2003) *Early Childhood Professionals: Leading Today and Tomorrow*. Sydney: MacLennan and Petty.

Education Act (1996). London: HMSO.

End of Poverty Campaign (2008) *Unhealthy Lives*. London: End Poverty Campaign and GMB.

Every Child Matters: Change for Children (2004). London: Department for Education and Skills.

Every Parent Matters (2006) Nottingham: Department Children Schools Families Publications.

Firestone, W. and Riehl, C. (2005) *A New Agenda for Research in Educational Leadership (Critical Issues in Educational Leadership)*. New York: Teachers College Press.

Department of Health, Department for Employment & Education, Home Office (2000), Framework for the Assessment of Children in Need. London, The Stationery Office.

Fullan, M. (2001) *Leading in a Culture of Change*. San Francisco: Jossey-Bass.

Ghate, D. and Hazel, N. (2002) *Parenting in Poor Environments*. London: Jessica Kingsley.

Gold. A. and Evans, J. (1998) *Reflecting on School Management*. London: Falmer Press.

Goldschmied, E. and Jackson, S. (2004) *People Under Three, Young Children in Daycare* (Second edition). Routledge: London and New York.

Guardian (2008) Editorial, 3 Dec., p. 23.

Hall, V. (1996) *Dancing on the Ceiling: A Study of Women Managers in Education*. London: Paul Chapman.

Harris, A. and Lambert, L. (2003) *Building Leadership Capacity for School Improvement*. Maidenhead: Open University Press.

Heller, R. (1999) *Managing Change*. London: Dorling Kindersley Publishing.

Herzberg, F., Mausner, B. and Snyderman, B. (1993) *The Motivation to Work*. London: Transaction Publishers.

High Scope Educational Research Foundation, www.highscope.org, accessed 5.02.09.

Hoff, E., Laursen, B. and Tardif, T. (2002) 'Socioeconomic status and parenting', in M. Bornstein (ed.) *Handbook of Parenting*, Vol. 2 (Second edition). London: Lawrence Erlbaum Associates.

Johnson, S. (1709–84), www.samueljohnson.com. accessed 10.02.09.

Kagan, S. L. and Hallmark, L. G. (2001) 'Cultivating leadership in early care and education', *Childcare Education Exchange*, 140: 7–10.

Kao, R. Y. W. (1986) *Entrepreneurship, Creativity and Organisation*. NJ: Prentice Hall.

Kets de Vries, M. (2001) *Struggling with the Demon, Perspectives on Organisational and Individual Irrationality*. Connecticut: International Universities Press.

Kolb, D. (1984) *Experiential Learning Styles*. Englewood Cliffs, NJ: Prentice Hall.

Kotter, J. (1988) *The Leadership Factor*. New York: Collier MacMillan.

Kouzes, J. and Posner, B. (1999) *Encouraging the Heart: A Leader's Guide to Rewarding and Recognizing Others*. San Francisco: Jossey-Bass.

Laevers, F. (2004) *Involvement of Teacher and Children Style: Insight from an Inter- national Study on Experiential Learning*. Leuven, Belgium: University of Leuven.

Lambert, L. (1998) *Building Leadership Capacity in Schools*. Alexandria, VA: USA Association of Supervision and Curriculum Development.

Larkin, E. (2008) *Ready to Lead*. London: Pearson Education.

Leadbeater, C. (1997) *The Rise of the Social Entrepreneur*. London: Demos.

Lee, W, Carr, M, Soutar, M., Mitchell, L. (2013) *Understanding the Te Whāriki Approach*, Routledge David Fulton Book.

Local Government Charity Toolkit, http://www.charity-commission.gov.uk/enhancingcharities/toolindex.asp

Leech, C. (2005) *Using Information for Decision Making*, revised by Corinne Leech. Oxford: Elsevier.

McClelland, D. (1961) *The Achieving Society*. Princeton, NJ: Van Nostrand.

Malaguzzi, L. (2005) *Reggio Children's Newsletter*, December 2005, p. 1.

Manning, M. and Haddock, P. (1989) *Leadership Skills for Women*. USA: Crisp Publications. Inc.

Marconi, G. (1874–1937) www.wikipedia.org, accessed 23.01.09.

Maslow. A. (1998) *Maslow on Management*, NY: Wiley and Sons.

Mawson, A. (2008) *The Social Entrepreneur*. London: Atlantic Books.

Melhuish, E. and Belsky J. and Leyland, A. (2008) *The Impact of Sure Start Local Programmes on three Year Olds and their Families*. Report 027. Institute of Study for Social Issues, Children, Families and Communities. Birkbeck, University London. DfES Publications Nottingham

Meltzer, H. and Gatward, R., with Goodman, R. and Ford, T. (2000) *Mental Health of Children and Adolescents in Great Britain*. London: The Stationery Office.

Moyles, J. (2007) *Effective Leadership and Management in the Early Years*. Maidenhead: Open University Press.

Muijs, D., Aubrey, C., Harris, A., and Briggs, M (2004) 'How do they manage? A review of the research on leadership in early childhood', *Journal of Early Childhood Research*, 2(2):157–160.

National College for School Leadership (2005), 'Think Tank Report for the Governing Body of the National College of School Leadership' by Prof David Hopkins, NCSL University of Nottingham. http://www.ncsl.org.uk, accessed 10 Feb. 2009.

National Family and Parenting Institute (2000)

NCVO : http://www.ncvo-vol.org.uk/askncvo/trusteegovernance/?id=757, accessed 31 May 2009.

Ofsted Annual Review (2000) London: The Stationery Office.

Ofsted (2008a) *Early Years Foundation Stage*. London: HMSO.

Ofsted (2008b) *Early Years: Leading to Excellence*. London: HMSO.

Ofsted (2013) *Unseen Children: Access and Achievement 20 Years On*. London: HMSO.

Ogden-Newton, A. (2007) *2020 Vision*. London: Social Enterprise, June, p. 2

Organization for Economic Cooperation and Development (2006) *Starting Strong 11/12, Early Childhood Education and Care*. Paris: OECD Publishing Office.

Putnam, R. (2000) *Bowling Alone*. New York: Simon & Schuster.

Qualification Curriculum Authority (2000) *Curriculum Guidance for the Foundation Stage*. London: QCA.

Ratcliffe, S. (ed.) (2000) *Quotations by Subject*. Oxford: Oxford University Press.

Reggio Emilia *Municipal Infant-Toddlers Centres and Pre-Schools*. http://zer-osei.comune.re.it/inter/index.htm, accessed 5.02.09.

Robb, C. (2007) *Social Enterprise Plan for London*. Office of the Third Sector.

Rodd, J. (1996) *Leadership in Early Childhood: The Pathway to Professionalism*. Melbourne: Allen & Unwin.

Rodd, J. (1997) 'Learning to be leaders: perceptions of early childhood professionals about leadership roles and responsibilities', *Early Years*, 18(1)

Rodd, J. (1998) *Leadership in Early Childhood* (2nd edition). Pub loc: Open University

Roffey Park (2005) *Self Managed Development*. Ashridge

Roffey Park Management Agenda (2008) *Personnel Today*, 12 Feb., p. 47.

Saint Exupéry, Antoine de (1954). *The Wisdom of the Sands*, trans. S. Gilbert from the French *Citadelle*. London: Hollis and Carter. Quote taken from www.brai-nyquotes.com/quotes.

Sargent, H. (1978) *Fishbowl Management: Participation Approach to Management*. Wiley and Sons Inc.

Scottish Government (2010) *Growing up in Scotland: Maternal mental health and its impact on child behaviour and development*. Edinburgh: HMSO.

Shea, M. (1990) *Leadership Rules*. London: Century.

Sinclair, I. (2006) '0–5: How Small Children Make A Big Difference', Provocation Series 3, 1, *The Work Foundation*.

Siraj-Blatchford, I. and Mani, L. (2007) *Effective Leadership in the Early Years*. London: Institute of Education.

Social Care Institute for Excellence Report (2008) 'Proven Practice', *Community Carer*, 10 June: 22.

Starting Strong 11: Early Childhood Education and Care (2006) OECD.

Stogdill, R.M. (1974) *Handbook of Leadership*. New York: Free Press.

Sykes, G. (1996) Reform of and as Professional Leader. Phi Kappan Delta.

Sylva, K. (1999) 'Effective Provision of Pre-School Education (EPPE) Project, Technical Paper', *6 Characteristics of the Centres in the EPPE Sample: Observational Profiles*. London: Institute of Education, University of London.

Sylva, K. (2004) *Provision of Pre-School Education (EPPE) Project, Final Report*. London: Institute of Education, University of London.

Te Whāriki (2001) *Early Years Curriculum* Wellington: Ministry of Education, Learning Media.

Tichy, N. (2004) *The Cycle of Leadership: How Great Leaders Teach their Com- panies to Win*. US Harper Business.

Timmons, J. (1994) *New Venture Creation: A Guide to Entrepreneurship* (Second edition). Homeward, ILL: Richard D. Irwin Inc.

Tomlinson, H. (2004) *Educational Leadership*. London: Sage Publications.

Turner, K., Sands, M. and Markie-Dadds, C. (1999) *Practitioners' Manual for Primary Care: Triple P*, University of Queensland

UNICEF (2007) An overview of child well-being in rich countries, http://www.unicef.org/media/files/ChildPovertyReport.pdf

Utting, W. (1995) *Children and Violence*. Report of the Commission on Children and Violence. UK Gulbenkian Foundation.

Waniganayake, M., Morda, R. and Kapsalakis, A. (2000) 'Leadership in child care centre: Is it just another job?' Special Issue: Management and Leadership, *Australian Journal of Early Childhood* 28(1): 13–19.

Weatherburn, D. and Lind, B. (2001) *Deliquent-prone Communities*. Melbourne: Cambridge University Press.

Weisbord, S. and Janoff, M. (2000) *Future Search: An Action Guide to Finding Common Ground in Organisations and Communities*. San Francisco: Berrett– Koehler.

Whitaker, P. (1993) *Managing Change in Schools*. Buckingham: Open University Press.

Whiteley, P. Director of the Economic Social Research Council (ESRC) *Democracy and Participation Programme*. www.esrc.ac.uk, accessed 27.01.15.

Winnicott, D. (1987) *The Child, the Family and the Outside World*. Cambridge: Perseus.

www.charity-commission.gov.uk, accessed 27.01.15.

Index